PRACTICE - ASSESS - DIAGNOSE

180 Days of HIGH-FREQUENCY WORDS for First Grade

Author
Jodene Smith, M.A.

SHELL EDUCATION

For information on how this resource meets national and other state standards, see page 4. You may also review this information by visiting our website at www.teachercreatedmaterials.com/administrators/correlations/ and following the on-screen directions.

Publishing Credits

Corinne Burton, M.A.Ed., *Publisher*; Conni Medina, M.A.Ed., *Managing Editor*; Emily R. Smith, M.A.Ed., *Content Director*; Angela Johnson, M.A.Ed., M.F.A., *Editor*; Lee Aucoin, *Senior Multimedia Designer*; Don Tran, *Production Artist;* Kyleena Harper, *Assistant Editor*

Image Credits

All images from iStock and Shutterstock.

Standards

Shell Education
A division of Teacher Created Materials
5301 Oceanus Drive
Huntington Beach, CA 92649-1030

http://www.tcmpub.com/shell-education

ISBN 978-1-4258-1634-6

Printed by: 926. Printed in: Malaysia. PO#: PO16423

TABLE OF CONTENTS

INTRODUCTION AND RESEARCH

If you teach early learners to read, you know how important the mastery of high-frequency words is to reading success. Students who are exposed to and learn high-frequency words during these critical years of academia set the foundation for reading and overall success as scholars. The words in this book make up "65% of written material" that we encounter on a daily basis and are the connective tissues used to craft even the simplest written sentence (Fry 2000, 4).

The Need for Practice

To be successful in today's classroom, students must be able to accurately identify and read high-frequency words. Building accuracy and fluency when reading these words is critical for later reading success mainly because, unlike other words, "some of these often-used words do not follow regular phonics rules" (Fry 2000, 4). Being able to read these words allows students to focus on fluency instead of decoding while reading. The National Reading Panel suggests that repeated exposure to high-frequency words is crucial to reading instruction and sets the building blocks for decoding, fluency, and comprehension (2000). According to Robert Marzano, "practice has always been, and always will be, a necessary ingredient to learning procedural knowledge at a level at which students execute it independently" (2010, 83).

Understanding Assessment

In addition to providing opportunities for frequent practice, teachers must be able to assess students' acquisition of high-frequency words. This is important for teachers to adequately support students' progress in fluency and comprehension. Assessment is a long-term process that often involves careful analysis of students' responses from discussions, projects, practice sheets, and tests. In short, the data gathered from assessments should be used to inform instruction: slow down, speed up, or reteach. This type of evaluation is called *formative assessment* (McIntosh 1997).

HOW TO USE THIS BOOK

180 Days of High-Frequency Words for First Grade offers weekly units to guide students as they practice and learn words every day of the school year. Each daily activity is designed to engage students with the words of the week. On the first day, students are introduced to the words of the week. For the rest of the week, students complete activities in which they must **recognize**, **play with**, **use**, and **write** the words of the week.

Easy to Use and Standards Based

The Every Student Succeeds Act (ESSA) mandates that all states adopt challenging academic standards that help students meet the goal of college and career readiness. While many states already adopted academic standards prior to ESSA, the act continues to hold states accountable for detailed and comprehensive standards. These daily activities reinforce grade-level skills and allow students to read, write, speak, and listen to high-frequency words every day of the school year. This chart indicates reading, writing, language, and print concept standards that are addressed throughout this book.

Reading—phonics and word recognition	Read common high-frequency words by sight.
	Distinguish between similarly spelled words by identifying the sounds of the letters that differ.
	Add drawings or other visual displays to descriptions as desired to provide additional detail.
Writing—text type and purpose	Use a combination of drawing, dictating, and writing to compose informative/explanatory texts in which students name what they are writing about and supply some information about the topic.
Language—conventions of standard English	Demonstrate command of the conventions of standard English grammar and usage when writing or speaking.
	Print many uppercase and lowercase letters.
	Use frequently occurring nouns and verbs.
	Produce and expand complete sentences in shared language activities.
	Demonstrate command of the conventions of standard English capitalization, punctuation, and spelling when writing.
	Capitalize the first word.
	Spell simple words phonetically, drawing on knowledge of sound-letter relationships.
Print concepts	Demonstrate understanding of the organization and basic features of print.
	Follow words from left to right, top to bottom, and page by page.
	Recognize that spoken words are represented in written language by specific sequences of letters.
	Understand that words are separated by spaces in print.

HOW TO USE THIS BOOK *(cont.)*

Using the Practice Pages

Practice pages provide instruction for each day of the school year. Teachers may wish to prepare packets of weekly practice pages for the classroom or for homework. As outlined on page 4, every page is aligned to phonics skills and word recognition skills.

The week starts with introductory activities. The focus for the first half of the week is to familiarize students with the words of the week.

Each day of the week focuses on a new skill. There are five overarching skills used in this book: introducing, recognizing, playing, using, and writing with the words. See page 7 for detailed objectives for each day.

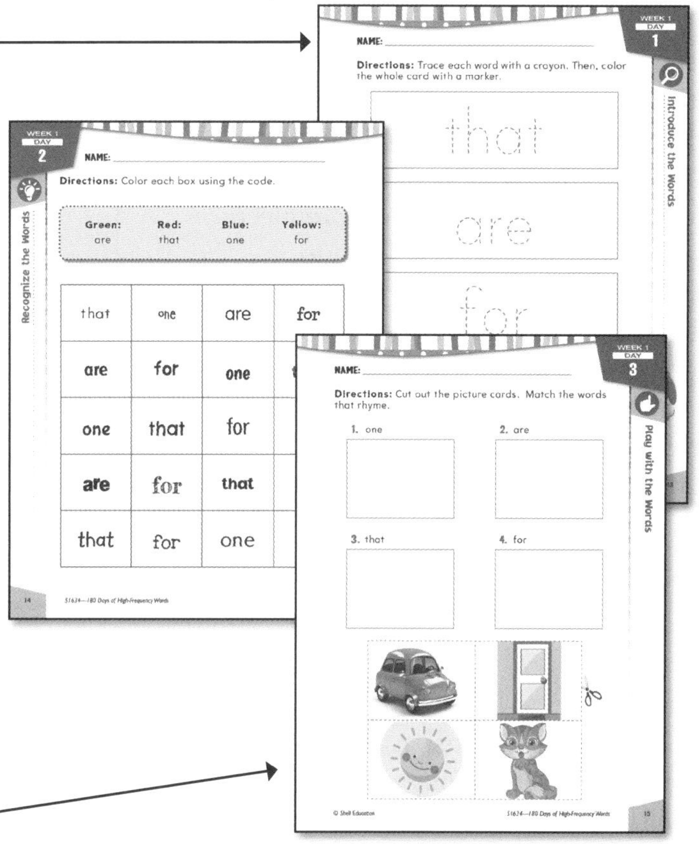

Each week students explore new words through kinesthetic activities.

At the end of the week, students read and write using the high-frequency words of the week. For a detailed explanation of each activity, see pages 8–9.

Using the Resources

The student extension activities, assessment materials, and flash cards in this book are available as digital PDFs and Microsoft Word® documents online. A complete list of the available documents is provided on page 216. To access the Digital Resources, go to: www.tcmpub.com/download-files. Enter this code: 89107477. Follow the on-screen directions.

The quarterly assessment tools will aid the classroom teacher in tracking the high-frequency words your class recognizes throughout the year. The checklist on page 11 should be reproduced for each student in the class. Use it to record the words students recognize each quarter. Use page 12 to log students' progress throughout the year. This page can be used to see, at a glance, common high-frequency words that still need additional practice, as well as trends to drive whole-class instruction.

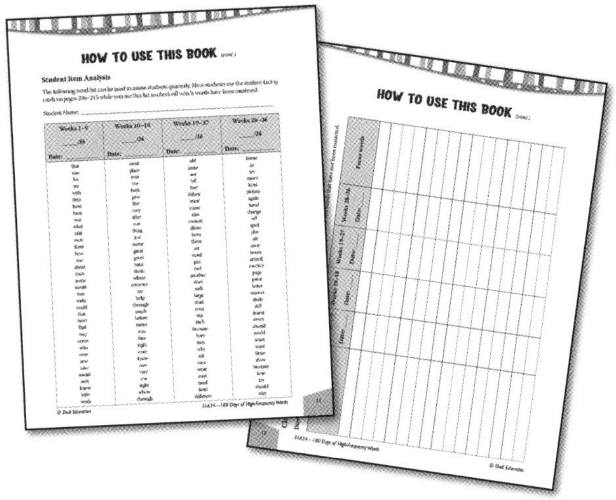

HOW TO USE THIS BOOK (cont.)

Student Item Analysis

HOW TO USE THIS BOOK (cont.)

Pages 198–205 can be used for home/school connection extension activities. The games and suggestions are engaging and will help students practice reading and identifying all of the high-frequency words in this book.

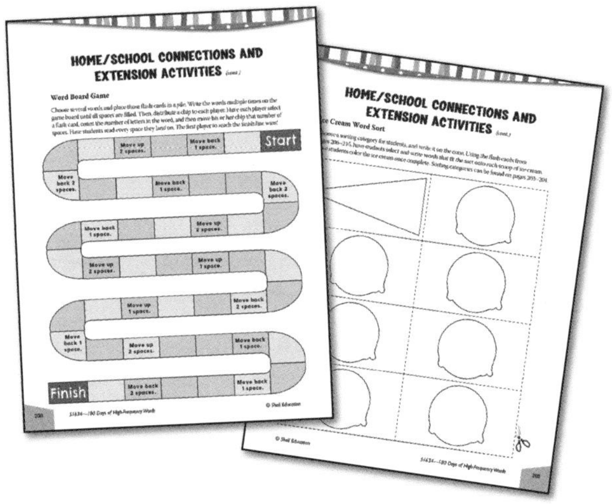

HOME/SCHOOL CONNECTIONS AND EXTENSION ACTIVITIES (cont.)

Word Board Game

HOME/SCHOOL CONNECTIONS AND EXTENSION ACTIVITIES (cont.)

Dr. Edward Fry created a list of 1,000 Instant Words to teach children. That list was used in choosing the words for this series. On pages 206–215, the words from Fry's list that are used in this book are provided as flash cards. These cards can be used as a tool for the quarterly assessments. Additionally, these flash cards can used with the home/school connection and extension activities.

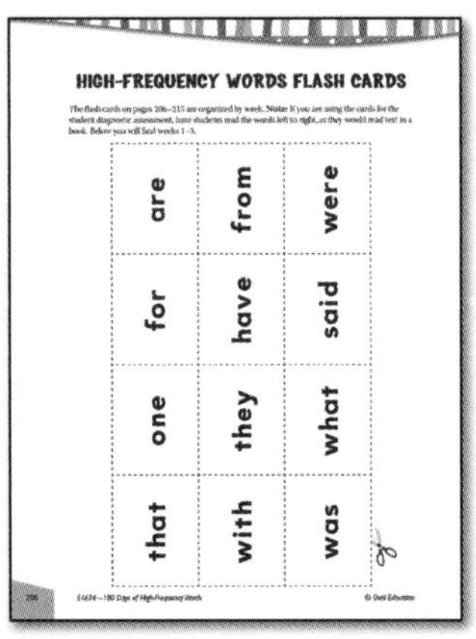

HIGH-FREQUENCY WORDS FLASH CARDS

are	from	were
for	have	said
one	they	what
that	with	was

HOW TO USE THIS BOOK *(cont.)*

For 180 days, educators can use this book to support students' acquisition and recognition of high-frequency words. The book is divided into 36 weeks, with five days of activities per week. Each week, students are introduced to three high-frequency words. The format of the week is as follows: introduce the words, recognize the words, play with the words, use the words, and write the words.

Below is a list of daily activities. Detailed descriptions for each activity can be found on pages 8–9.

Daily Description	Names of Activities
Day 1—Introduce the Words For the first day of each week, students complete introductory activities. These activities are designed to introduce and familiarize students with the high-frequency words of the week. Students create flash cards with the high-frequency words. These can be stored in a zip-top bag at each student's desk or taken home as a study tool for the week.	Crayon Relief Flash Cards Making Flash Cards Snap and Spell Flash Cards
Day 2—Recognize the Words The second day of each week is devoted to recognition activities. Activities are designed around identifying the high-frequency words of the week written in multiple fonts and styles.	Color by Word Font Match Word Shapes
Day 3—Play with the Words On day three, students play with the words of the week. These activities are geared toward tactile manipulation of the high-frequency words. These activities infuse play, art, and hands-on activities for the week.	Rhyming Words Telephone Math Game Word Clues Word Sort
Day 4—Use the Words On the fourth day of the week, students use the words of the week in context. Students tell or write stories using the words, or act as word detectives and read the words.	Create Sentences Fill in the Sentence Finish Sentences Read and Color Use and Color
Day 5—Write the Words On day five, students engage in writing activities. Using the high-frequency words of the week, students craft stories and illustrations. These activities motivate all students to apply what they have learned during the week.	Word Story Mixed-up Sentences Fill in the Sentences

HOW TO USE THIS BOOK *(cont.)*

Below is a detailed explanation and rationale for each activity in *180 Days of High-Frequency Words for First Grade.*

Activity	Description
Color by Word	Students practice recognizing the high-frequency words of the week in various fonts by coloring words using color codes.
Crayon Relief Flash Cards	Students trace the letters on the flash cards with crayons and then color over the whole flash card with markers. The result is a crayon relief. It is especially fun to use a white crayon when doing this activity.
Create Sentences	Students describe scenes with sentences using high-frequency words. Students can do this activity orally. If they are more advanced or later in the year, have students write the sentences on separate pieces of paper. Encourage students to create stories about the pictures once they are more comfortable doing this activity.
Fill in the Sentence	After cutting out the high-frequency words of the week, students match them to appropriate sentences. Then, students practice reading sentences to partners.
Finish Sentences	Cloze sentences are provided into which students must insert the correct words. Students complete simple sentence stems that contain the high-frequency words. Then, students illustrate one of the cloze sentences.
Font Match	After cutting out cards with the high-frequency words shown in various fonts, students acquaint themselves to the various ways the words can look by sorting the words.
Making Flash Cards	Similar to the Crayon Relief Flash Cards activity, students trace the lines of the letters on the flash cards with a marker. For this activity students are given creative license to decorate the rest of the card as they please. Consider using glitter, salt, small pasta, or cotton balls that have been stretched.
Mixed-up Sentences	Students are provided with the words to a sentence; however, they are all mixed up. Students must rearrange the words to create sentences and then draw pictures.
Read and Color	Students match pictures and simple sentences using the high-frequency words.
Rhyming Words	Students focus on making rhymes by matching pictures and words or words and words.

HOW TO USE THIS BOOK *(cont.)*

Activity	Description
Snap and Spell Flash Cards	This activity provides a kinesthetic way for students to interact with the letters in the words. Tall letters (letters that touch the top line) stretch up high to the blue sky and are traced with blue. Short letters (letters that touch the mid-line) are level with the grass and are traced with green. Low letters (letters that go below the bottom line) go down in the dirt and are traced with brown. After students understand the colors that represent the height of each letter, have them snap and spell their words. Students stand, and as they say the names of the letters, they snap their hands in the appropriate places: over their heads for tall letters, at their waists for short letters, and down by their toes for low letters.
Telephone Math Game	Students are given the words of the week and a telephone keypad. Students have to make one-to-one correlation with each letter with the number assigned to the telephone keypad. Students then add all numbers that correspond with the letters in each word to get a sum.
Use and Color	Students read the words of the week used in sentences. Students need to find and circle the high-frequency word in each sentence and then color the picture that illustrates each sentence.
Word Clues	Provided word cards are matched to the corresponding clues to practice high-frequency words.
Word Shapes	Students focus on the shapes of the words in this activity. The shapes or outlines of the words are provided. Students must match the correct words to the shapes. Then, they write the words again on the provided lines and draw the outlines of the shapes of the words.
Word Sort	Categories that the high-frequency words fit into are provided. Students must sort the words into the categories. Some words may fit into more than one category.
Word Story	Simple stories using the high-frequency words are provided. Students must complete the cloze sentences in order to complete the stories, and then draw pictures.

HOW TO USE THIS BOOK *(cont.)*

Diagnostic Quarterly Assessment

Teachers can use the *Student Item Analysis Checklist* to monitor students' learning. This tool can enable teachers or parents to quickly score students' work and monitor students' progress. Teachers and parents can see which high-frequency words students know and which ones they do not.

The words in this book are divided into four list. Each list can be used to assess students quarterly throughout the year. The *Student Item Analysis Checklist* on page 11 should be used by the teacher to administer the assessment. The *High-Frequency Word Flash Cards* on pages 207–215 should be used as the student-facing list. Below you will find detailed steps to administer each component of the diagnostic assessment.

To Complete the Student Item Analysis Checklist:

- Write or type the student's name on the name line at the top of the chart. One copy per student is needed to track his or her ongoing progress throughout the year.
- Give each student the flash cards that correspond with the *Student Item Analysis Checklist* on page 11. Use the *Student Item Analysis Checklist* to mark students' responses. Students should be able to identify each word in a few seconds.
- The numbers across the top of the chart can be used to log each student's percentage of correct words in each quarter of the school year. For each quarter, record how many high-frequency words each student is able to accurately identify.

To Complete the Class Item Analysis:

- After each student has completed a list from the *Student Item Analysis Checklist,* use the *Class Item Analysis* chart on page 12 to log the results. Write or type students' names in the far-left column. Depending on the number of students in your class, more than one copy of the form may be needed, or you may need to add rows.
- Indicated across the top of the chart are the weeks that correspond with each word list. Students are assessed every 9 weeks.
- For each student, record his or her score in the appropriate column.
- Students' scores can be placed in the middle columns and scored by averaging the number of words in the week compared to the words identified correctly. Place the results in the correct column. Use these scores as benchmarks to determine how students are performing. This allows for four benchmark assessments during the year that can be used to gather formative diagnostic data. Use the last column to identify trends in the classroom for additional high-frequency lesson planning.

HOW TO USE THIS BOOK *(cont.)*

Student Item Analysis

The following word list can be used to assess students quarterly. Have students use the student-facing cards on pages 206–215 while you use this list to check off which words have been mastered.

Student Name: ____

Weeks 1–9 _____/36 Date: __________	Weeks 10–18 _____/36 Date: __________	Weeks 19–27 _____/36 Date: __________	Weeks 28–36 _____/36 Date: __________
that	most	old	home
one	place	same	us
for	year	any	try
are	me	tell	move
with	back	boy	kind
they	give	follow	picture
have	live	want	again
from	very	came	hand
was	after	also	change
what	our	around	off
said	thing	show	spell
were	just	farm	play
there	name	three	air
how	great	set	away
use	good	small	house
about	man	put	animal
their	think	end	mother
some	where	another	page
would	sentence	does	point
two	say	well	letter
write	help	large	answer
could	through	must	study
first	much	even	still
been	before	big	found
find	mean	such	every
may	too	because	should
come	line	here	world
who	right	turn	learn
over	over	why	want
new	know	ask	three
take	new	men	show
sound	very	went	because
only	our	read	here
know	right	need	try
little	where	land	should
work	through	different	why

Class Item Analysis

Directions: Record students' quarterly progress on the chart. Use the last column to record words that have not been mastered.

Student Name	Weeks 1–9 Date: ____	Weeks 10–18 Date: ____	Weeks 19–27 Date: ____	Weeks 28–36 Date: ____	Focus words

NAME: ______________________________

Directions: Trace each word with a crayon. Then, color the whole card with a marker.

that
are
for
one

Recognize the Words

NAME: ____________________

Directions: Color each box using the code.

Green:	**Red:**	**Blue:**	**Yellow:**
are	that	one	for

that	one	are	for
are	for	one	that
one	that	for	are
are	for	that	one
that	for	one	are

NAME: ______________________________

Directions: Cut out the picture cards. Match the words that rhyme.

1. one

2. are

3. that

4. for

NAME: ____________________

Directions: Read each sentence. Circle the word of the week found in each sentence. Color the pictures.

that one for are

1. We are happy.

2. He has one dog.

3. That is my cat.

4. This is for you.

NAME: ______________________________

Directions: Finish the story using the words. Draw a picture to match.

that one for are

Sam and Tom ____________ friends.

Sam has ____________ apple.

The apple is ____________ Tom.

____________ made Tom happy.

NAME: ____________________

Directions: Trace each word with a marker. Then, decorate each card.

with

they

have

from

Recognize the Words

NAME: ______________________________

Directions: Cut out the word cards. Glue the cards in the right columns to match the words.

with	they	have	from

with	have	they	from
have	from	with	they

Play with the Words

NAME: ______________________________

Directions: Cut out the word cards. Match the word cards and the clues.

1. This word has a short *i* sound.
2. This word begins with *th.*
3. The last letter in this word is an *e*.
4. This word rhymes with *come*.

with	they
have	from

NAME: ______________________________

Directions: Cut out the word cards. Finish each sentence using the correct word.

1. I will go [ ] you.

2. Where are you [ ] ?

3. Do you [ ] some water?

4. [ ] can tell time.

with	They
have	from

NAME: ____________________

Write the Words

Directions: Read the sentence. Write the sentence two times. Cut out the word cards, and glue them in the box to form the sentence.

They have a friend with them.

have	with	them.	They	friend	a

NAME: ______________________________

Directions: Trace tall letters with a blue crayon. Trace short letters with a green crayon. Trace low letters with a brown crayon. Then, snap and spell each word.

was

what

said

were

Recognize the Words

NAME: ______________________________

Directions: Write the word that fits in each word shape. Then, write the word on the line.

was   said   what   were

Example: boy

1. 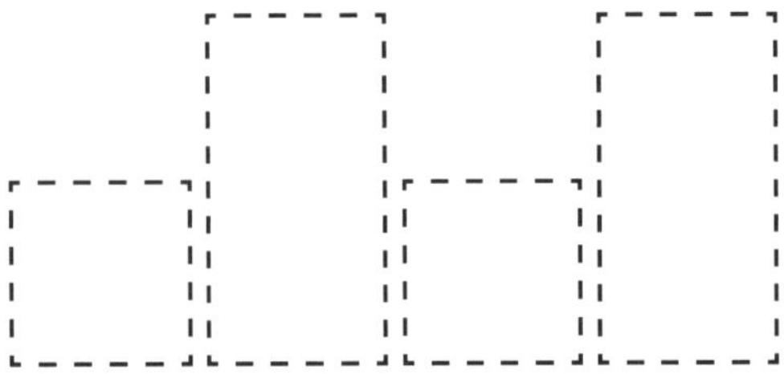 ______________

2.  ______________

3.  ______________

4.  ______________

NAME: ______________________________

Directions: Cut out the word cards. Place each card in the correct space. **Hint**: A word can only be in a column once.

Words that begin with *w*	Words that have the letter *a*	Words that have four letters

was	was	said
said	what	what
were	were	what

NAME: ______________________________

Directions: Make up a story about the pictures using the words. Tell a friend your story.

was	said	what	were

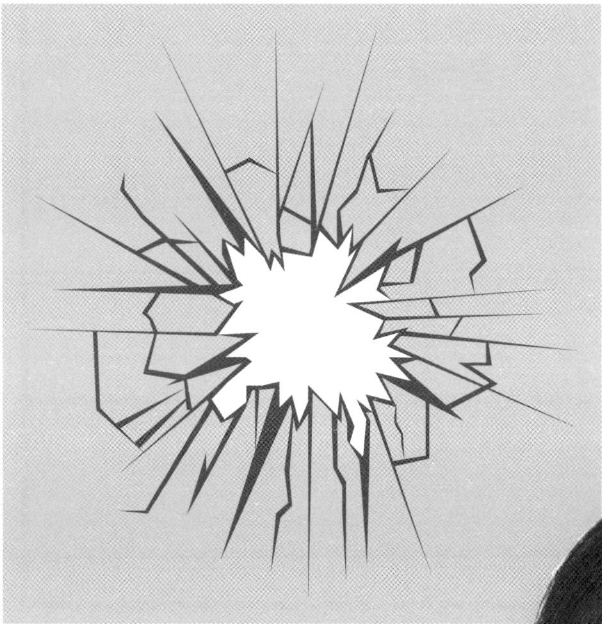

NAME: ______________________________

Directions: Finish each sentence with one of the words. Read each sentence.

was	said	what	were

1. We ______________ going to the movies.

2. ______________ should we see?

3. I ______________, "Let's see a funny movie."

4. Dad ______________ happy about that.

NAME: ______________________________

Directions: Trace each word with a crayon. Then, color the whole card with a marker.

there

use

how

about

NAME: ____

Directions: Color each box using the code.

Green:	Red:	Blue:	Yellow:
about	use	how	there

about	use	how	how
there	how	there	about
use	there	about	use
about	how	use	there
there	use	how	about

NAME: ______________________________

Directions: Cut out the picture cards. Match the words that rhyme.

1. about

2. how

3. there

4. use

NAME: ______________________________

Directions: Read each sentence, and circle the word of the week. Color the pictures.

there   use   how   about

1. Look over there!

2. The book is about a cat.

3. How many are inside?

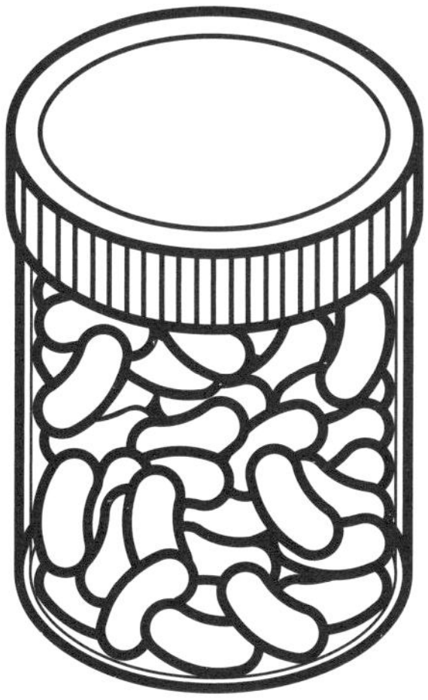

4. I use this to open a can.

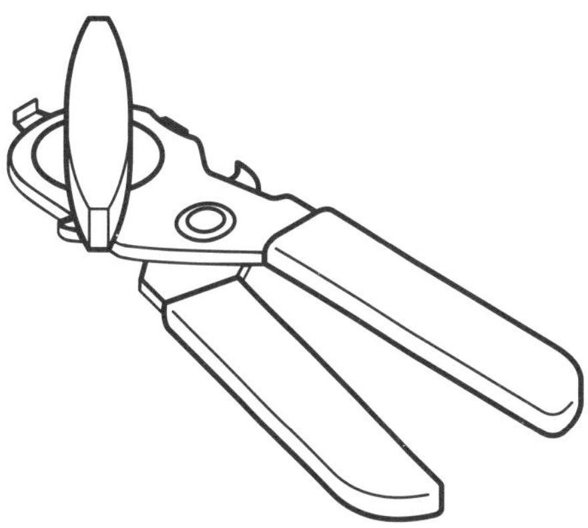

Write the Words

NAME: ____________________

Directions: Finish the story using the words. Draw a picture to match.

about how use there

______ is a man.

He will ______ a pen.

He will write ______ numbers.

He will show ______ to add.

NAME: ______________________________

Directions: Trace each word with a marker. Then, decorate each card.

their

some

two

would

NAME: ______________________________

Recognize the Words

Directions: Cut out the word cards. Glue the cards in the right columns to match the words.

some	would	their	two

would	their	some	two
some	two	their	would

NAME: ____

Directions: Cut out the word cards. Match the word cards and the clues.

1. This word is a number. [ ]

2. This word rhymes with *should*. [ ]

3. This word has five letters. [ ]

4. This word has a silent *e*. [ ]

their	some
would	two

Use the Words

NAME: ____________________

Directions: Cut out the word cards. Finish each sentence using the correct word.

1. I need [ ] more time.

2. The kids and [ ] mom are in the car.

3. My little sister is [ ] years old.

4. [ ] you like to come?

their	some
Would	two

NAME: ______________________________

Directions: Read the sentence. Write the sentence two times. Cut out the word cards, and glue them in the box to form the sentence.

Two girls would like some milk.

like	milk.	Two	girls	some	would

NAME: ______________________________

Directions: Trace tall letters with a blue crayon. Trace short letters with a green crayon. Trace low letters with a brown crayon. Then, snap and spell each word.

write

first

could

been

NAME: ______________________________

Directions: Write the word that fits in each word shape. Then, write the word on the line.

been first write could

Example: girl

1.

2.

3.

4.

Play with the Words

NAME: ______________________________

Directions: Cut out the word cards. Place each card in the correct space. **Hint**: A word can only be in a column once.

Words that have five letters	Words that end with the /*t*/ sound	Words that have two vowels

could	write	first
write	could	been
first	write	

NAME: ______________________________________

Directions: Make up a story about the picture below using the words. Tell a friend your story.

been first write could

Write the Words

NAME: ______________________________

Directions: Finish each sentence with one of the words. Read each sentence aloud.

been   first   write   could

1. I will ______________ a story about my aunt.

2. ______________ you pass me the book?

3. I have ______________ to the park.

4. She came in ______________. I came in second.

NAME: ______________________________

Directions: Trace each word with a crayon. Then, color the whole card with a marker.

find

come

may

what

Recognize the Words

NAME: ______________________________

Directions: Color each box using the code.

Green:	**Red:**	**Blue:**	**Yellow:**
find	who	may	come

who	come	find	who
may	who	may	find
find	come	come	may
come	may	find	who
may	find	who	come

NAME: ______________________________

Directions: Cut out the picture cards. Match the words that rhyme.

1. who

2. may

3. come

4. find

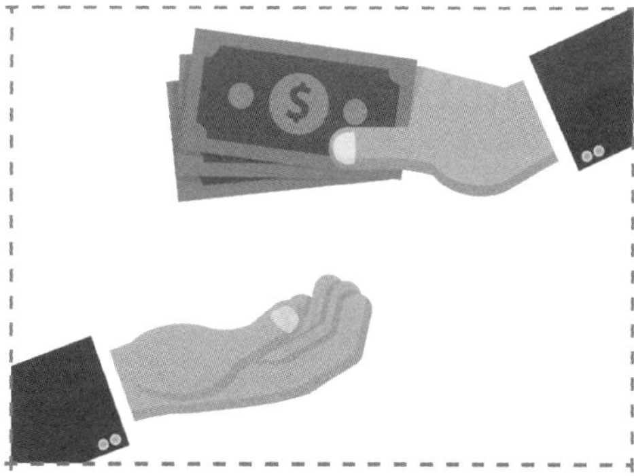

NAME: ______________________________

Directions: Read each sentence, and circle the word of the week. Color the pictures.

come	who	find	may

1. Who wants to go for a ride?

2. Come on in!

3. She will find the boy.

4. May I play?

NAME: ____________________

Directions: Finish the story using the words. Draw a picture to match.

who may come find

My friends will ____________ to my party.

____________ wants to play?

____________ I be *it*?

____________ me!

NAME: ______________________________

Directions: Trace each word with a marker. Then, decorate each card.

over

take

new

sound

NAME: ________________________________

Directions: Cut out the word cards. Glue the cards in the right columns to match the words.

over	sound	take	new

over	new	take	over
sound	take	sound	new

NAME: ______________________________

Play with the Words

Directions: Cut out the word cards. Match the word cards and the clues.

1. This word has three letters.

2. This word is the opposite of *under*.

3. This word has five letters.

4. This word rhymes with *bake*.

take	sound
over	new

NAME: ____________________

Use the Words

Directions: Cut out the word cards. Finish each sentence using the correct word.

1. I have a [ ] hat.

2. Go [ ] the hill.

3. Can I [ ] one?

4. What is that [ ]?

take	new
sound	over

NAME: ____________________

Write the Words

Directions: Read the sentence. Write the sentence two times. Cut out the word cards, and glue them in the box to form the sentence.

He will take the new car.

new	He	take	the	will	car.

NAME: ____

Directions: Trace tall letters with a blue crayon. Trace short letters with a green crayon. Trace low letters with a brown crayon. Then, snap and spell each word.

only

little

know

work

Recognize the Words

NAME: ______________________

Directions: Write the word that fits in each word shape. Then, write the word on the line.

work little know only

Example: c a t

1\.

2\.

3\.

4\.

NAME: ____

Directions: Cut out the word cards. Place each card in the correct space. **Hint**: A word can only be in a column once.

Words that have two syllables	Words that have the letter *o*	Words that have the long /*o*/ sound

know	only	only
work	know	
only	little	

Use the Words

NAME: ____

Directions: Make up a story about the picture below using the words. Tell a friend your story.

work	little	know	only

NAME: ______________________________

Directions: Finish each sentence with one of the words. Read each sentence aloud.

work	little	know	only

1. I have a ______________ sister.

2. She is ______________ three years old.

3. We ______________ on art projects together.

4. I ______________ it will look great!

Introduce the Words

NAME: ____________________

Directions: Trace each word with a crayon. Then, color the whole card with a marker.

most

year

place

me

NAME: ____________________

Directions: Color each box using the code.

Green:	**Red:**	**Blue:**	**Yellow:**
place	most	me	year

place	me	year	most
most	year	place	me
year	me	most	year
place	most	me	place
me	most	place	most

NAME: ____

Directions: Cut out the picture cards. Match the words that rhyme.

1. place

2. year

3. most

4. me

NAME: ____

Directions: Read each sentence, and circle the word of the week. Color the pictures.

me most place year

1. It's me!

2. Have a Happy New Year!

3. Who has the most books?

4. He came in first place.

Write the Words

NAME: ______________________________

Directions: Finish the story using the words. Draw a picture to match.

place   me   year   most

Last ____________ I took a trip.

I went to a fun ____________.

I saw the ____________ people I had ever seen!

It was fun for ____________.

NAME: ______________________________

Directions: Trace each word with a marker. Then, decorate each card.

back

give

live

very

NAME: ______________________________

Directions: Cut out the word cards. Glue the cards in the right columns to match the words.

very	give	live	back

give	very	very	back
live	back	give	live

NAME: ____________________

Directions: Cut out the word cards. Match the word cards and the clues.

1. These two words rhyme.

2. This word ends with the /*k*/ sound.

3. This word has a *y* that makes the long *e* sound.

very	give
live	back

NAME: ______________________________

Directions: Cut out the word cards. Finish each sentence using the correct word.

1. I like that part ____________ much!

2. Will she come ____________ soon?

3. I ____________ in a house.

4. I should ____________ this to her.

give	back
live	very

NAME: ______________________________

Directions: Read the sentence. Write the sentence two times. Cut out the word cards, and glue them in the box to form the sentence.

Give me one from the back.

one	from	Give	the	me	back.

NAME: ______________________________

Directions: Trace tall letters with a blue crayon. Trace short letters with a green crayon. Trace low letters with a brown crayon. Then, snap and spell each word.

after

thing

our

just

NAME: ____________________

Directions: Write the word that fits in each word shape. Then, write the word on the line.

our thing after just

Example: d o g

1. ____________________

2. ____________________

3. ____________________

4. ____________________

Play with the Words

NAME: ______________________________

Directions: Cut out the word cards. Place each card in the correct space. **Hint**: A word can only be in a column once.

our thing after just

Words that have five letters	Words that have one syllable	Words that end with *r*

our	after	
just	thing	
thing	after	our

NAME: ____

Directions: Make up a story about the picture below using the words. Tell a friend your story.

our thing after just

NAME: ____________________

Directions: Finish each sentence with one of the words. Read each sentence aloud.

thing	after	our	just

1. This is ____________ tent.

2. ____________ the sun goes down, we will make a fire.

3. We ____________ have to wait for mom.

4. What is this ____________?

NAME: ______________________________

Directions: Trace each word with a crayon. Then, color the whole card with a marker.

name

good

great

man

Recognize the Words

NAME: ______________________________

Directions: Color each box using the code.

Green:	**Red:**	**Blue:**	**Yellow:**
good	name	man	great

name	great	good	name
man	name	man	great
great	good	name	man
good	man	great	good
man	good	man	great

NAME: ______________________________

Directions: Cut out the picture cards. Match the words that rhyme.

1. name

2. good

3. man

4. great

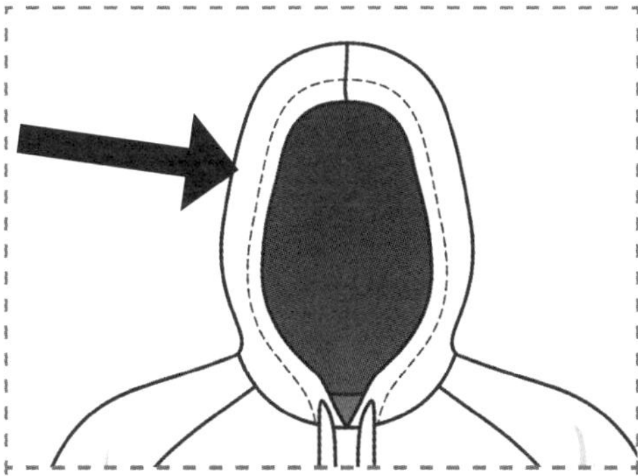

NAME: ______________________________

Directions: Read each sentence. Circle the word from the Word Bank. Then, color each picture.

great	man	name	good

1. The man can write.

2. She had a good time.

3. It is a great day.

4. His name is Tim.

NAME: ______________________

Directions: Finish the story using the words. Draw a picture to match.

man	name	great	good

It was a ____________ day.

No, it was a ____________ day!

I read about a well-known ____________.

His ____________ was Abraham Lincoln.

NAME: ____

Directions: Trace each word with a marker. Then, decorate each card.

think

where

sentence

say

NAME: ____

Directions: Cut out the word cards. Glue the cards in the right columns to match the words.

think	say	sentence	where

think	sentence	where	say
sentence	where	say	think

Play with the Words

NAME: ____________________

Directions: Cut out the word cards. Match the word cards and the clues.

1. This word has five letters but only four sounds.

2. This word has two vowels that are the same.

3. This word ends with the long *a* sound.

4. This word has eight letters.

think	sentence
where	say

NAME: ______________________________

Directions: Cut out the word cards. Finish each sentence using the correct word.

1. I know how to write a [ ] .

2. What did you [ ] ?

3. I wonder, [ ] do you live?

4. I [ ] I am right!

say	think
sentence	where

NAME: ______________________

Directions: Read the sentence. Write the sentence two times. Cut out the word cards, and glue them in the box to form the sentence.

Where do you think she went?

she	do	where	you	think	went?

NAME: ______________________________

Directions: Trace tall letters with a blue crayon. Trace short letters with a green crayon. Trace low letters with a brown crayon. Then, snap and spell each word.

help

through

before

much

NAME: ____________________

Recognize the Words

Directions: Write the word that fits in each word shape. Then, write the word on the line.

before through help much

Example: toy

1.

2.

3.

4.

NAME: ______________________________

Directions: Cut out the word cards. Place each card in the correct space. **Hint**: A word can only be in a column once.

Words that have four letters	Words that have one syllable	Words that have silent letters

before	through	help
much	through	
much	help	

NAME: ______________________________

Directions: Make up a story about the picture below using the words. Tell a friend your story.

before	through	help	much

NAME: ____________________

Directions: Finish each sentence with one of the words. Read each sentence aloud.

before through help much

1. There is too ____________ work!

2. Do you need any ____________?

3. I can help you ____________ I start reading.

4. Thank you for helping me get ____________ it.

NAME: ______________________________

Directions: Trace each word with a crayon. Then, color the whole card with a marker.

mean

line

too

right

NAME: ______________________________

Directions: Color each box using the code.

Green:	**Red:**	**Blue:**	**Yellow:**
right	mean	too	line

right	too	line	mean
mean	line	right	line
too	mean	mean	too
right	line	too	right
too	right	line	too

Play with the Words

NAME: ____________________

Directions: Cut out the picture cards. Match the words that rhyme.

1. line

2. right

3. too

4. mean

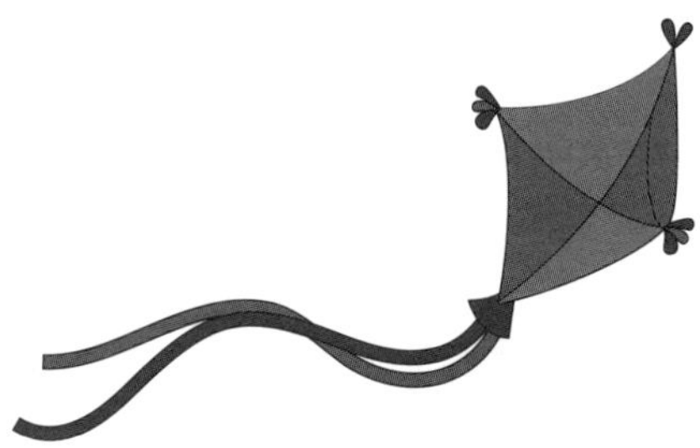

NAME: ______________________________

Directions: Read each sentence. Draw a line to connect the picture with the sentence. Circle and write the word.

line too mean right

1. Make a right turn.

2. He is a boy too!

3. That dog looks mean.

4. Can you trace a line?

NAME: ____________________

Directions: Finish the story using the words. Draw a picture to match.

right	mean	too	line

I got in ____________.

A ____________ girl cut in front of me.

My friend smiled and made it ____________.

The girl smiled, ____________.

NAME: ____________________

Directions: Trace each word with a marker. Then, decorate each card.

over

new

know

very

NAME: ______________________________

Recognize the Words

Directions: Cut out the word cards. Glue the cards in the right columns to match the words.

over	new	know	very

over	know	new	very
new	very	over	know

NAME: ______________________________

Directions: Cut out the word cards. Match the word cards and the clues.

1. This word sounds like the word *no*.

2. This word has three letters.

3. The last letter in this word is *y*.

4. This word is the opposite of *under*.

over	very
know	new

NAME: ______________________________

Use the Words

Directions: Cut out the word cards. Finish each sentence using the correct word.

1. Come [ ] here.

2. Is that a [ ] car?

3. I love you [ ] much!

4. Do you [ ] him?

over	very
know	new

NAME: ______________________________

Directions: Read the sentence. Write the sentence two times. Cut out the word cards, and glue them in the box to form the sentence.

I like the new dog very much!

I	dog	new	the	very	like	much!

NAME: ____

Directions: Trace tall letters with a blue crayon. Trace short letters with a green crayon. Trace low letters with a brown crayon. Then, snap and spell each word.

our

where

right

through

NAME: ____________________

Directions: Write the word that fits in each word shape. Then, write the word on the line.

where right our through

Example: s h o w

1.

2.

3.

4.

Play with the Words

NAME: ____________________

Directions: Read each word. Write the words in the correct column. **Hint**: A word can only be in a column once.

our through right where

Words that have *gh*	Words that have two vowels	Words that have five letters

NAME: ____

Directions: Make up a story about the picture below using the words. Tell a friend your story.

where	right	our	through

NAME: ______________________

Directions: Finish each sentence with one of the words. Read each sentence aloud.

where	right	our	through

1. I write with my ______________ hand.

2. We went ______________ the sliding doors.

3. ______________ did I put my notebook?

4. Mom brought ______________ dog to the park.

NAME: ______________________________

Directions: Trace each word with a marker. Then, decorate each card.

old

any

same

tell

NAME: ____________________________________

Directions: Cut out the word cards. Glue the cards in the right columns to match the words.

old	tell	same	any

any	tell	old	same
tell	same	any	old

NAME: ______________________________

Directions: Cut out the word cards. Match the word cards and the clues.

1. This word has a silent *e*.

2. This word has a *y* that sounds like long *e*.

3. This word has two letters that are the same.

4. This word is the opposite of *new*.

tell	any
same	old

Use the Words

NAME: ____________________

Directions: Cut out the word cards. Finish each sentence using the correct word.

1. Who can I [ ] ?

2. They both look the [ ] !

3. Do you want [ ] more?

4. The tree is [ ] .

tell	any
same	old

NAME: ______________________________

Directions: Read the sentence. Write the sentence two times. Cut out the word cards, and glue them in the box to form the sentence.

Tell me, are there any old books?

are	there	Tell	old	any	books?	me,

NAME: ______________________________

Directions: Trace tall letters with a blue crayon. Trace short letters with a green crayon. Trace low letters with a brown crayon. Then, snap and spell each word.

boy

follow

came

want

NAME: ____

Directions: Write the word that fits in each word shape. Then, write the word on the line.

want came follow boy

1. ______________________

2. ______________________

3. ______________________

4. ______________________

Play with the Words

NAME: ______________________________

Directions: Read each word. Write the words in the correct column. **Hint**: A word can only be in a column once.

want   came   follow   boy

Words that have four letters	Words that have one syllable	Words that have two vowels

NAME: ____

Directions: Make up a story about the picture below using the words. Tell a friend your story.

want   came   follow   boy

Write the Words

NAME: ______________________________

Directions: Find and circle each word. Be creative and finish each sentence.

follow	came	want	boy

1. I want ______________________________.

2. That boy ______________________________.

3. She came from ______________________________.

4. Follow me ______________________________.

NAME: ____

Directions: Trace each consonant with a blue marker. Trace each vowel with a red marker. Then, color the whole card with a crayon.

show

also

farm

around

Recognize the Words

NAME: ____________________

Directions: Cut out the word cards. Glue the cards in the right columns to match the words.

farm	around	show	also

also	farm	show	farm
around	show	around	also

NAME: ____

Directions: Create categories for a word sort. Place the words in the correct column. **Hint**: A word can only be in a column once.

also   around   farm   show

Category Suggestions: number of letters, number of vowels, number of syllables, silent letters, begins/ends with...

NAME: ____________________

Directions: Cut out the picture cards. Match each sentence and picture.

around also show farm

1. Let me show you my room.

2. He will stop at the corner.

3. We went to the farm.

4. She will go along also.

NAME: ______________________________

Directions: Read the sentence. Write the sentence two times. Cut out the word cards, and glue them in the box to form the sentence.

He will show me around the farm.

He	show	farm.	the	will	me	around

Introduce the Words

NAME: ______________________________

Directions: Trace each *e* blue. Trace each *l* brown. Trace each *t* green. Trace the rest of the letters orange. Then, decorate each card.

three

set

put

small

Recognize the Words

NAME: ____________________

Directions: Write the word that fits in each word shape. Then, write the word on the line, and draw the word shape around the word.

set small three put

1. ____________________

2. ____________________

3. ____________________

4. ____________________

NAME: ______________________________

Directions: The words of the week are hidden in code. Use the phone to break the code.

set small three put

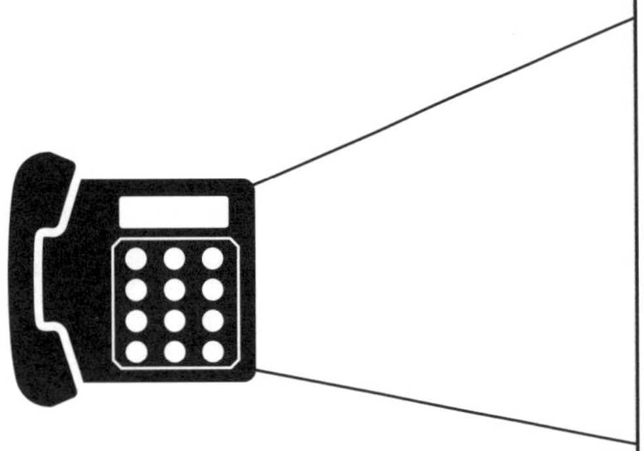

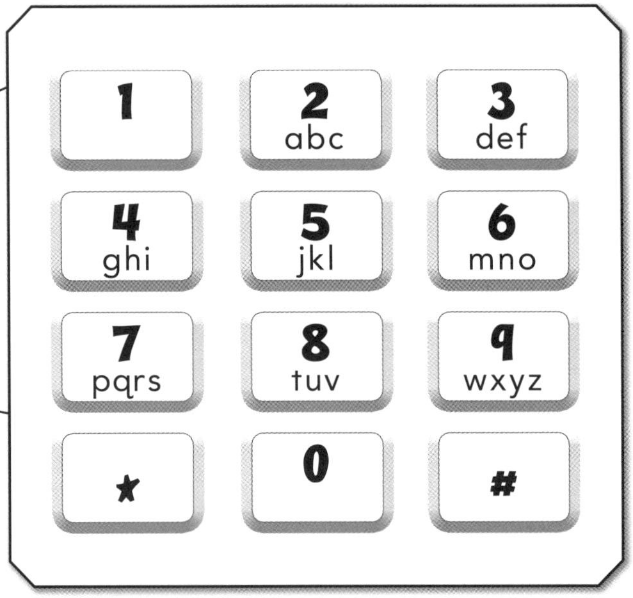

Example: 2 + 2 + 8 = 12
cat

1. 7 + 8 + 8

____

2. 7 + 3 + 8

____

3. 7 + 6 + 2 + 5 + 5

____

4. 8 + 4 + 7 + 3 + 3

____

Use the Words

NAME: ____________________

Directions: Write your own sentences for the words. Leave the words of the week out. Have a friend solve each sentence.

Example: I ___ate___ a banana.

set small three put

1. ______________________________

______________________________.

2. ______________________________

______________________________.

3. ______________________________

______________________________.

4. ______________________________

____

Write the Words

NAME: ______________________________

Directions: Write one sentence using as many words from the Word Bank as you can. Draw a picture to match your sentence.

set	small	three	put

NAME: ______________________________

Directions: Trace tall letters with a blue crayon. Trace short letters with a green crayon. Trace low letters with a brown crayon. Then, snap and spell each word.

does

end

another

well

Directions: Turn the page over, and write the words two more times without looking at the words.

Recognize the Words

NAME: ______________________________

Directions: Color each box using the code. Then, tally the number of times you found each word.

Green:	**Red:**	**Blue:**	**Yellow:**
does	end	another	well

does	end	another	well
well	another	end	does
another	end	another	another
well	well	does	well

does	end	another	well

NAME: ______________________________

Directions: Write a clue for each word. Then, match the word cards and the clues.

1. This word is the opposite of ______________________.

2. This word has ____________ vowels next to each other.

3. This word has ____________ consonants that are the same.

4. This word has ____________ letters.

well	does
another	end

Use the Words

NAME: ____________________

Directions: Write about the picture below using the words.

well	another	does	end

NAME: ______________________________

Directions: Write sentences or a short story using the words. Draw a picture to match.

well   another   does   end

NAME: ______________________________

Directions: Trace each consonant with a blue crayon. Trace each vowel with a red crayon. Then, color the whole card with a marker.

large

even

must

big

NAME: ______________________________

Directions: Write the word that fits in each word shape. Then, write the word on the line, and draw the word shape around the word.

big large must even

1. 

2. 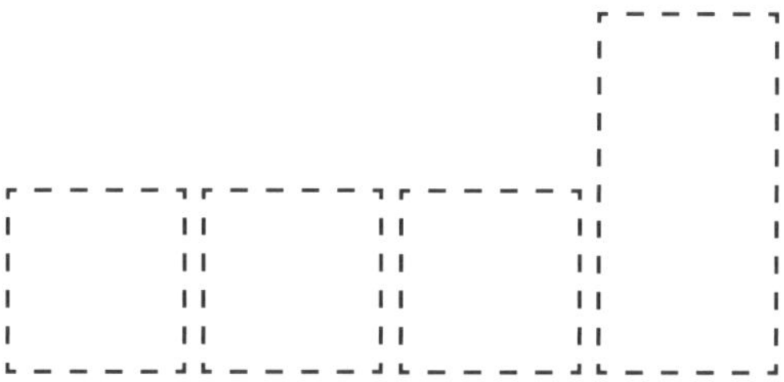

3. 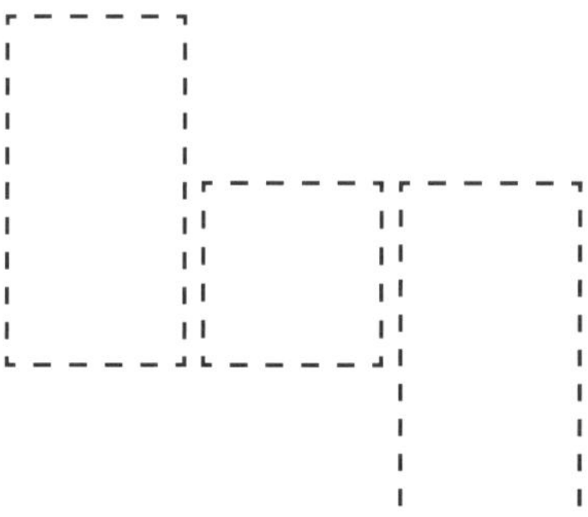

4. 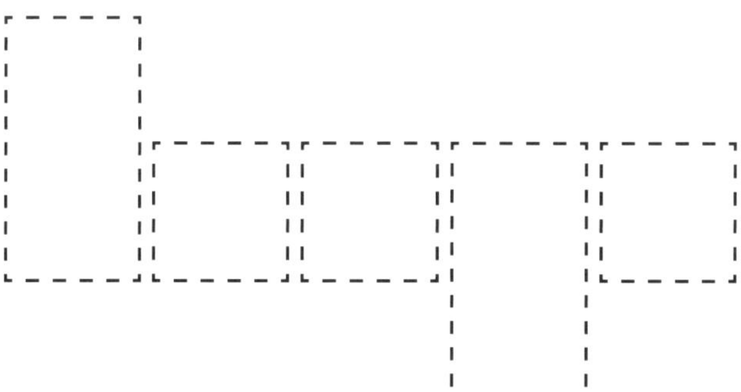

NAME: ____________________

Directions: The words of the week are hidden in code. Use the phone to break the code.

big large must even

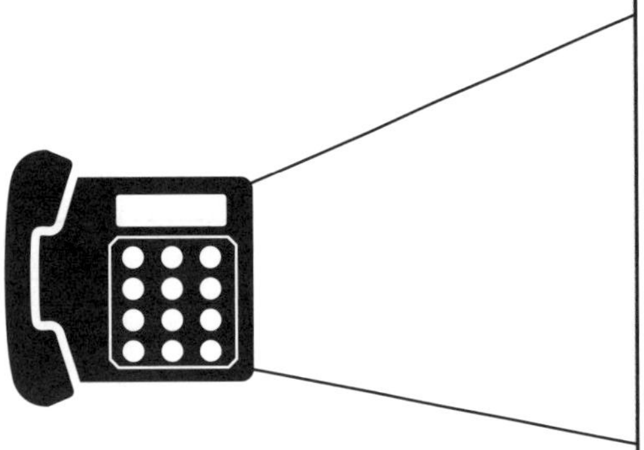

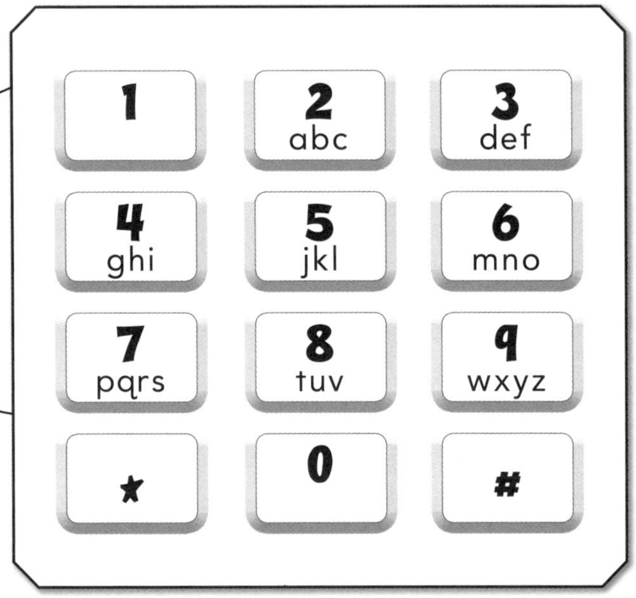

Example: 3 + 6 + 4 = 13
dog

1. 6 + 8 + 7 + 8

____

2. 2 + 4 + 4

____

3. 3 + 8 + 3 + 6

____

4. 5 + 2 + 7 + 4 + 3

____

NAME: ______________________________

Directions: Write your own sentences for the words. Leave the words of the week out. Have a friend solve each sentence.

Example: I like bananas.

big	large	must	even

1. ______________________________.

2. ______________________________.

3. ______________________________.

4. ______________________________.

NAME: ______________________________

Directions: Write one sentence using as many words from the Word Bank as you can. Draw a picture to match your sentence.

big	large	must	even

NAME: ______________________________________

Directions: Trace each *c* and *h* green. Trace each *e* and *u* purple. Trace each *s* and *r* blue. Trace the rest of the letters brown. Then, decorate each card.

such

here

because

turn

Directions: Turn over each flash card and write the words two more times without looking at the front.

Recognize the Words

NAME: ______________________

Directions: Color each box using the code. Then, tally the number of times you found each word.

Green:	**Red:**	**Blue:**	**Yellow:**
here	because	turn	such

because	here	such	here
here	such	because	such
because	here	such	because
turn	because	here	here

here	because	turn	such

NAME: ______________________________

Directions: Write a clue for each word. Then, match the word cards and the clues.

1. This word has __________ vowels that are the same.

2. This word has __________ letters.

3. This word ends with __________.

4. This word begins with __________.

such	because
turn	here

NAME: ______________________________

Use the Words

Directions: Write about the picture below using the words.

such turn here because

NAME: ______________________________

Directions: Write sentences or a short story using the words. Draw a picture to match.

such turn here because

NAME: ______________________________

Directions: Trace tall letters with a blue crayon. Trace short letters with a green crayon. Trace low letters with a brown crayon. Then, snap and spell each word.

why

men

ask

went

Directions: Turn over each flash card and write the words two more times without looking at the front.

NAME: ____

Directions: Cut out the word cards. Glue the cards in the right columns to match the words.

why	men	ask	went

Recognize the Words

Directions: Write each word using your own fun font.

went	men	ask	why
ask	why	men	went

Play with the Words

NAME: ______________________________

Directions: Create categories for a word sort. Write the words in the correct column. **Hint**: A word can only be in a column once.

why men ask went

Category Suggestions: number of letters, number of vowels, number of syllables, silent letters, begins/ends with...

NAME: ______________________________

Directions: Cut out the picture cards. Match each sentence and picture.

why men ask went

1. The men are happy.

2. She will ask for a cookie.

3. We went on a trip.

4. Why are you happy?

Write the Words

NAME: ____________________

Directions: Read the sentence. Write the sentence two times. Cut out the word cards, and glue them in the box to form the sentence.

The men went to ask for food.

to	men	food.	ask	The	for	went

NAME: ______________________________

Directions: Trace each consonant with a blue crayon. Trace each vowel with a red crayon. Then, color the whole card with a marker.

read

land

need

different

Directions: Turn over each flash card and write the words two more times without looking at the front.

NAME: ____________________

Directions: Write the word that fits in each word shape. Then, write the word on the line, and draw the word shape around the word.

land different need read

1.

2.

3.

4.

NAME: ______________________________

Directions: Write a clue for each word. Then, match the word cards and the clues.

1. ______________________________

2. ______________________________

3. ______________________________

4. ______________________________

need	read
land	different

Use the Words

NAME: ______________________________

Directions: Write about the picture below using the words.

land different need read

____

____

____

NAME: ____________________

Directions: Write sentences or a short story using the words. Draw a picture to match.

land different need read

Introduce the Words

NAME: ____________________

Directions: Trace each *e* with a purple marker. Trace each *m* with a red marker. Trace the rest of the letters black. Then, decorate each card.

home

try

us

move

Directions: Turn over each flash card and write the words two more times without looking at the front.

NAME: ____

Directions: Color each box using the code. Then, tally the number of times you found each word.

Green:	**Red:**	**Blue:**	**Yellow:**
us	move	home	try

home	try	us	us
try	us	home	home
us	move	try	us
try	us	move	try

home	move	try	us

NAME: ____________________

Play with the Words

Directions: Create categories for a word sort. Write the words in the correct column. **Hint**: A word can only be in a column once.

home try move us

Category Suggestions: number of letters, number of vowels, number of syllables, silent letters, begins/ends with...

NAME: ____

Directions: Cut out the picture cards. Match each sentence and picture.

1. She is at home.

3. It is for us.

2. He will try some.

4. He can move the box.

NAME: ____________________

Directions: Read the sentence. Write the sentence two times. Cut out the word cards, and glue them in the box to form the sentence.

They will move us to a new home.

us	They	will	to	new	move	home.	a

NAME: ______________________________

Directions: Trace tall letters with a blue crayon. Trace short letters with a green crayon. Trace low letters with a brown crayon. Then, snap and spell each word.

picture

kind

hand

again

Directions: Turn over each flash card and write the words two more times without looking at the front.

NAME: ____________________

Directions: Cut out the word cards. Glue the cards in the right columns to match the words.

again	picture	hand	kind

Directions: Write each word using your own fun font.

hand	again	kind	again
kind	picture	hand	picture

NAME: ____________________

Directions: The words of the week are hidden in code. Use the phone to break the code.

again	picture	hand	kind

Example: 8 + 6 + 9 = 23
toy

1. 2 + 4 + 2 + 4 + 6

____

2. 7 + 4 + 2 + 8 + 8 + 7 +3

____

3. 4 + 2 + 6 + 3

____

4. 5 + 4 + 6 + 3

____

Use the Words

NAME: ______________________________

Directions: Write your own sentences for the words. Leave the words of the week out. Have a friend solve each sentence.

Example: Can I ___have___ a banana?

picture	hand	kind	again

1. ______________________________
______________________________.

2. ______________________________
______________________________.

3. ______________________________
______________________________.

4. ______________________________
______________________________.

NAME: ______________________________

Directions: Write sentences or a short story using the words. Draw a picture to match.

hand picture again kind

NAME: ____________________

Directions: Trace each consonant with a blue crayon. Trace each vowel with a red crayon. Then, decorate each card.

change

off

spell

play

Directions: Turn over each flash card and write the words two more times without looking at the front.

NAME: ______________________________

Directions: Write the word that fits in each word shape. Then, write the word on the line, and draw the word shape around the word.

change spell off play

1.

2.

3.

4.

NAME: ____________________

Directions: Write a clue for each word. Then, match the word cards and the clues.

1. ______________________________

2. ______________________________

3. ______________________________

4. ______________________________

change	off
play	spell

NAME: ______________________________

Directions: Cut out the picture cards. Match each sentence and picture.

off spell play change

1. They will go play.

3. I can spell cat.

2. He will turn the light off.

4. He got change after paying.

Write the Words

NAME: ____________________

Directions: Cut out the word cards to make a sentence. Write the sentence, then draw a picture to match.

She went off to play.

She	off	play.	to	went

NAME: ______________________________

Directions: Trace each *a* with an orange marker. Trace each *i* with a blue marker. Trace the rest of the letters with a green marker. Then, decorate each card.

air

house

away

animal

Directions: Turn over each flash card and write the words two more times without looking at the front.

Recognize the Words

NAME: ____

Directions: Color each box using the code. Tally the number of times you found each word.

Green:	**Red:**	**Blue:**	**Yellow:**
house	animal	away	air

animal	away	away	away
house	air	house	house
away	house	away	animal
house	away	animal	air

house	away	air	animal

NAME: ______________________________

Directions: Create categories for a word sort. Write the words in the correct column. **Hint**: A word can only be in a column once.

house animal air away

Category Suggestions: number of letters, number of vowels, number of syllables, silent letters, begins/ends with...

NAME: ____________________

Directions: Write your own sentences for the words. Leave the words of the week out. Have a friend solve each sentence.

Example: I want to ___eat___ a banana.

house animal air away

1. ______________________________.

2. ______________________________.

3. ______________________________.

4. ______________________________.

NAME: ___________________________

Directions: Write one sentence using as many words from the Word Bank as you can. Draw a picture to match your sentence.

air	house	away	animal

Introduce the Words

NAME: ____________________

Directions: Trace tall letters with a blue crayon. Trace short letters with a green crayon. Trace low letters with a brown crayon. Then, snap and spell each word.

mother

letter

point

page

Directions: Turn over each flash card and write the words two more times without looking at the front.

NAME: ______________________________________

Directions: Cut out the word cards. Glue the cards in the right columns to match the words.

point	mother	letter	page

Directions: Write each word using your own fun font.

point	letter	page	letter
page	mother	point	mother

NAME: ______________________________

Directions: The words of the week are hidden in code. Use the phone to break the code.

mother	page	letter	point

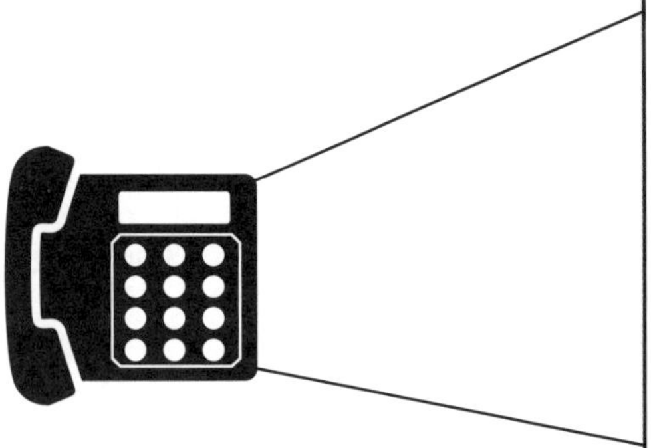

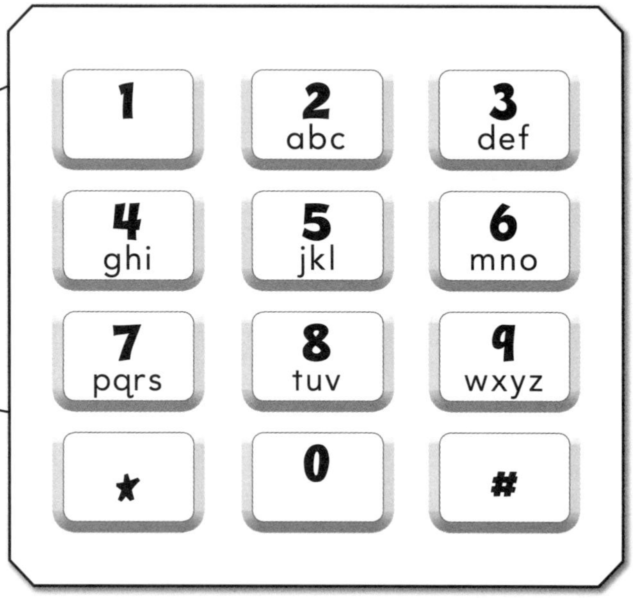

Example: 2 + 4 + 5 + 3 = 14
bike

1. 7 + 6 + 4 + 6 + 8

____

2. 6 + 6 + 8 + 4 + 3 + 7

____

3. 5 + 3 + 8 + 8 + 3 + 7

____

4. 7 + 2 + 4 + 3

____

NAME: ______________________________

Directions: Write about the picture below using the words.

mother   page   letter   point

Write the Words

NAME: ______________________________

Directions: Write sentences or a short story using the words. Draw a picture to match.

mother page letter point

NAME: ____

Directions: Trace each consonant with a blue crayon. Trace each vowel with a red crayon. Then, color the whole card with a marker.

answer

still

study

found

Directions: Turn over each flash card and write the words two more times without looking at the front.

Recognize the Words

NAME: ______________________

Directions: Write the word that fits in each word shape. Then, write the word on the line, and draw the word shape around the word.

still study found answer

1.

2.

3.

4.

NAME: ___________________________

Directions: Write a clue for each word. Then, match the word cards and the clues.

1. ___________________________

2. ___________________________

3. ___________________________

4. ___________________________

still	found
answer	study

Use the Words

NAME: ______________________________

Directions: Cut out the picture cards. Match each sentence and picture.

answer   found   study   still

1. She is still crying.

3. I found you!

2. He will give an answer.

4. She will study for the test.

NAME: ____________________

Directions: Write one sentence using as many words from the Word Bank as you can. Draw a picture to match your sentence.

still	found	answer	study

NAME: ____________________

Directions: Trace each word with a marker. Then, decorate each card.

every

world

should

learn

Directions: Turn over each flash card and write the words two more times without looking at the front.

NAME: ______________________________

Directions: Color each box using the code. Then, tally the number of times you found each word.

Green:	Red:	Blue:	Yellow:
world	should	every	learn

world	should	learn	every
should	learn	should	should
learn	every	world	learn
world	should	learn	should

every	learn	should	world

Play with the Words

NAME: ____________________

Directions: Create categories for a word sort. Write the words in the correct column. **Hint**: A word can only be in a column once.

learn every should world

Category Suggestions: number of letters, number of vowels, number of syllables, silent letters, begins/ends with...

Use the Words

NAME: ____________________

Directions: Write your own sentences for the words. Leave the words of the week out. Have a friend solve each sentence.

Example: Bananas are great!

learn every should world

1. ____________________.

2. ____________________.

3. ____________________.

4. ____________________.

Write the Words

NAME: ____________________

Directions: Write one sentence using as many words from the Word Bank as you can. Draw a picture to match your sentence.

learn	every	should	world

NAME: ____

Directions: Trace each consonant with a blue crayon. Trace each vowel with a red crayon. Then, color the whole card with a marker.

want

show

because

three

Directions: Turn over each flash card and write the words two more times without looking at the front.

Recognize the Words

NAME: ______________________

Directions: Cut out the word cards. Glue the cards in the right columns to match the words.

show	want	three	because

Directions: Write each word using your own fun font.

show	want	because	three
want	three	show	because

NAME: ____

Directions: Create categories for a word sort. Write the words in the correct column. **Hint**: A word can only be in a column once.

want   because   show   three

Category Suggestions: number of letters, number of vowels, number of syllables, silent letters, begins/ends with...

NAME: ______________________________

Directions: Cut out the picture cards. Match each sentence and picture.

1. She is three years old.

3. I want some, too!

2. He will show you the answer.

4. She stopped because she saw the sign.

NAME: ______________________________

Directions: Write one sentence using as many words from the Word Bank as you can. Draw a picture to match your sentence.

want	because	show	three

NAME: ____________________

Directions: Trace each word with a marker. Then, decorate each card.

should

try

here

why

Directions: Turn over each flash card and write the words two more times without looking at the front.

NAME: ______________________________

Directions: Write the word that fits in each word shape. Then, write the word on the line, and draw the word shape around the word.

why should here try

1. 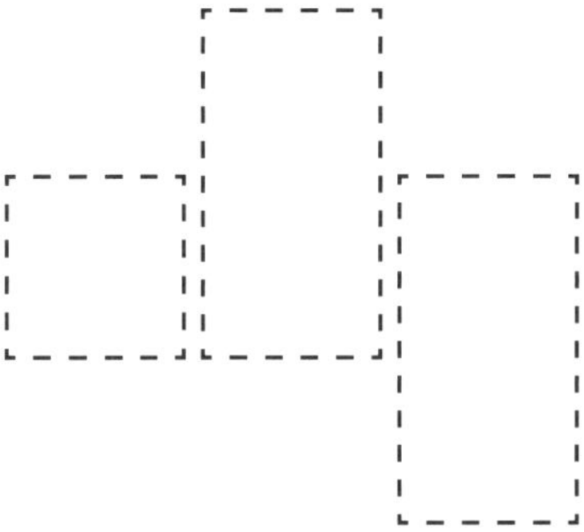

____

2. 

____

3. 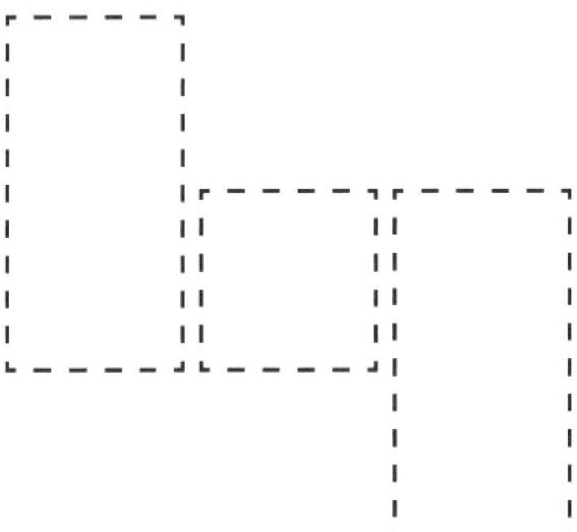

____

4. 

____

NAME: ______________________________

Directions: The words of the week are hidden in code. Use the phone to break the code.

here	should	try	why

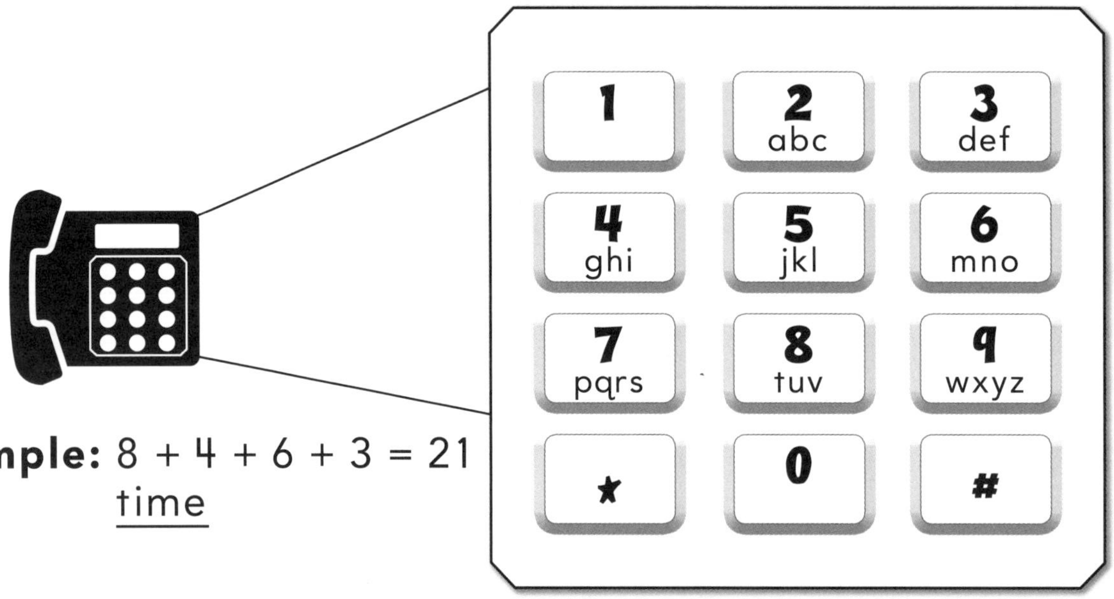

Example: 8 + 4 + 6 + 3 = 21
time

1. 8 + 7 + 9

____

2. 4 + 3 + 7 + 3

____

3. 7 + 4 + 6 + 8 + 5 + 3

____

4. 9 + 4 + 9

____

NAME: ____________________

Use the Words

Directions: Write your own sentences for the words. Leave the words of the week out. Have a friend solve each sentence.

Example: Can we go home?

why try here should

1. ____________________.

2. ____________________.

3. ____________________.

4. ____________________.

Write the Words

NAME: ____________________

Directions: Write one sentence using as many words from the Word Bank as you can. Draw a picture to match your sentence.

why	try	should	here

ANSWER KEY

The activity pages that do not have specific answers to them are not included in this answer key. Students' answers will vary on these activity pages, so check that students are staying on task.

Week 1: Day 3 (page 15)

1. sun
2. car
3. cat
4. door

Week 1: Day 4 (page 16)

1. are
2. one
3. That
4. for

Week 1: Day 5 (page 17)

Sam and Tom **are** friends. Sam has **one** apple. The apple is **for** Tom. **That** made Tom happy.

Week 2: Day 3 (page 20)

1. with
2. they
3. have
4. from

Week 2: Day 4 (page 21)

1. I will go **with** you.
2. Where are you **from**?
3. Do you **have** some water?
4. **They** can tell time.

Week 2: Day 5 (page 22)

They have a friend with them.

Week 3: Day 2 (page 24)

1. what
2. were
3. was
4. said

Week 3: Day 3 (page 25)

Words that begin with *w*	Words that have the letter *a*	Words that have four letters
was	was	said
what	said	what
were	what	were

Week 3: Day 5 (page 27)

1. We **were** going to the movies.
2. **What** should we see?
3. I **said**, "Let's see a funny movie."
4. Dad **was** happy about that.

Week 4: Day 3 (page 30)

1. shout
2. cow
3. bear
4. shoes

Week 4: Day 4 (page 31)

1. there
2. about
3. how
4. use

Week 4: Day 5 (page 32)

There is a man. He will **use** a pen. He will write **about** numbers. He will show **how** to add.

Week 5: Day 3 (page 35)

1. two
2. would
3. their
4. some

Week 5: Day 4 (page 36)

1. I need **some** more time.
2. The kids and **their** mom are in the car.
3. My little sister is **two** years old.
4. **Would** you like to come?

Week 5: Day 5 (page 37)

Two girls would like some milk.

Week 6: Day 2 (page 39)

1. first
2. write
3. been
4. could

Week 6: Day 3 (page 40)

Words that have five letters	Words that end with the /t/ sound	Words that have two vowels
could	first	been
first	write	write
write	could	

Week 6: Day 5 (page 42)

1. I will **write** a story about my aunt.
2. **Could** you pass me the book?
3. I have **been** to the park.
4. She came in **first**. I came in second.

Week 7: Day 3 (page 45)

1. shoe
2. pay
3. gum
4. blind

Week 7: Day 4 (page 46)

1. Who
2. Come
3. find
4. May

ANSWER KEY *(cont.)*

Week 7: Day 5 (page 47)

My friends will **come** to my party. **Who** wants to play? **May** I be *it*? **Find** me!

Week 8: Day 3 (page 50)

1. new
2. over
3. sound
4. take

Week 8: Day 4 (page 51)

1. I have a **new** hat.
2. Go **over** the hill.
3. Can I **take** one?
4. What is that **sound**?

Week 8: Day 5 (page 52)

He will take the new car.

Week 9: Day 2 (page 54)

1. only
2. know
3. work
4. little

Week 9: Day 3 (page 55)

Words that have two syllables	Words that have the letter *o*	Words that have the long /o/ sound
little	only	know
only	know	only
work		

Week 9: Day 5 (page 57)

1. I have a **little** sister.
2. She is **only** three years old.
3. We **work** on arts projects together.
4. I **know** it will look great!

Week 10: Day 3 (page 60)

1. vase
2. deer
3. ghost
4. tree

Week 10: Day 4 (page 61)

1. me
2. Year
3. most
4. place

Week 10: Day 5 (page 62)

Last **year** I took a trip. I went to a fun **place**. I saw the **most** people I had ever seen! It was fun for **me**.

Week 11: Day 3 (page 65)

1. give, live
2. back
3. very

Week 11: Day 4 (page 66)

1. I like that part **very** much!
2. Will she come **back** soon?
3. I **live** in a house.
4. I should **give** this to her.

Week 11: Day 5 (page 67)

Give me one from the back.

Week 12: Day 2 (page 69)

1. after
2. our
3. thing
4. just

Week 12: Day 3 (page 70)

Words that have five letters	Words that have one syllable	Words that end with *r*
thing	our	after
after	just	our
		thing

Week 12: Day 5 (page 72)

1. This is **our** tent.
2. **After** the sun goes down, we will make a fire.
3. We **just** have to wait for mom.
4. What is this **thing**?

Week 13: Day 3 (page 75)

1. game
2. hood
3. can
4. skate

Week 13: Day 4 (page 76)

1. man
2. good
3. great
4. name

Week 13: Day 5 (page 77)

It was a **good** day. No, it was a **great** day! I read about a well-known **man**. His **name** was Abraham Lincoln.

Week 14: Day 3 (page 80)

1. think
2. where
3. say
4. sentence

Week 14: Day 4 (page 81)

1. I know how to write a **sentence**.
2. What did you **say**?
3. I wonder, **where** do you live?
4. I **think** I am right!

Week 14: Day 5 (page 82)

Where do you think she went?

Week 15: Day 2 (page 84)

1. before
2. much
3. help
4. through

ANSWER KEY *(cont.)*

Week 15: Day 3 (page 85)

Words that have four letters	Words that have one syllable	Words that have silent letters
help	help	before
much	much	through
	through	

Week 15: Day 5 (page 87)

1. There is too **much** work!
2. Do you need any **help**?
3. I can help you **before** I start reading.
4. Thank you for helping me get **through** it.

Week 16: Day 3 (page 90)

1. nine
2. kite
3. glue
4. queen

Week 16: Day 4 (page 91)

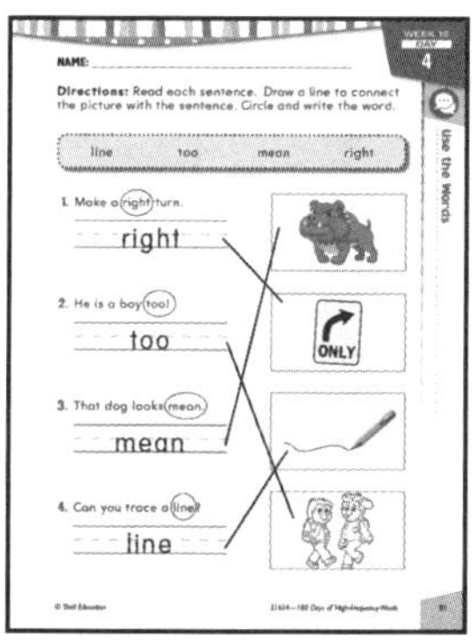

Week 16: Day 5 (page 92)

I got in **line**. A **mean** girl cut in front of me. My friend smiled and made it **right**. The girl smiled, **too**.

Week 17: Day 3 (page 95)

1. know
2. new
3. very
4. over

Week 17: Day 4 (page 96)

1. Come **over** here.
2. Is that a **new** car?
3. I love you **very** much!
4. Do you **know** him?

Week 17: Day 5 (page 97)

I like the new dog very much!

Week 18: Day 2 (page 99)

1. our
2. where
3. right
4. through

Week 18: Day 3 (page 100)

Words that have *gh*	Words that have two vowels	Words that have five letters
through	our	right
right	through	where
	where	

Week 18: Day 5 (page 102)

1. I write with my **right** hand.
2. We went **through** the sliding doors.
3. **Where** did I put my notebook?
4. Mom brought **our** dog to the park.

Week 19: Day 3 (page 105)

1. same
2. any
3. tell
4. old

Week 19: Day 4 (page 106)

1. Who can I **tell**?
2. They both look the **same**.
3. Do you want **any** more?
4. The tree is **old**.

Week 19: Day 5 (page 107)

Tell me, are there any old books?

Week 20: Day 2 (page 109)

1. boy
2. want
3. came
4. follow

Week 20: Day 3 (page 110)

Words that have four letters	Words that have one syllable	Words that have two vowels
want	boy	follow
came	want	came
	came	

Week 20: Day 5 (page 112)

1. want
2. boy
3. came
4. Follow

Week 21: Day 4 (page 116)

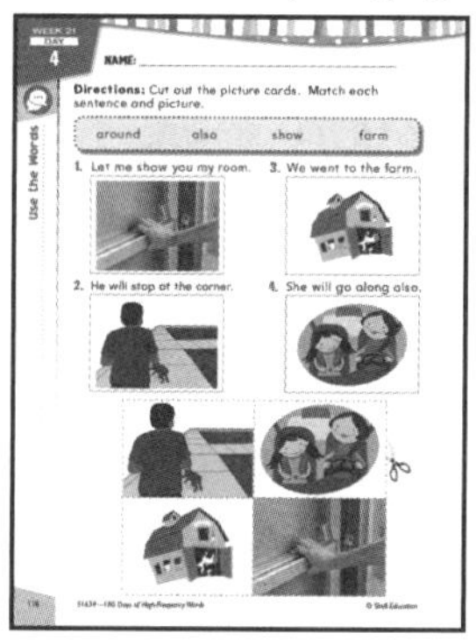

Week 21: Day 5 (page 117)

He will show me around the farm.

Week 22: Day 2 (page 119)

1. put
2. set
3. small
4. three

Week 22: Day 3 (page 120)

1. put
2. set
3. small
4. three

ANSWER KEY *(cont.)*

Week 23: Day 2 (page 124)

does	end	another	well
𝍷𝍷𝍷	𝍷𝍷𝍷	𝍸	𝍸

Week 24: Day 2 (page 129)

1. even
2. must
3. big
4. large

Week 24: Day 3 (page 130)

1. must
2. big
3. even
4. large

Week 25: Day 2 (page 134)

here	because	turn	such
𝍸𝍷	𝍸	𝍷	𝍷𝍷𝍷𝍷

Week 25: Day 3 (page 135)

1. This word has **two** vowels that are the same. (here)
2. This word has **seven** letters. (because)
3. This word ends with *h*. (such)
4. This word begins with *t*. (turn)

Week 26: Day 4 (page 141)

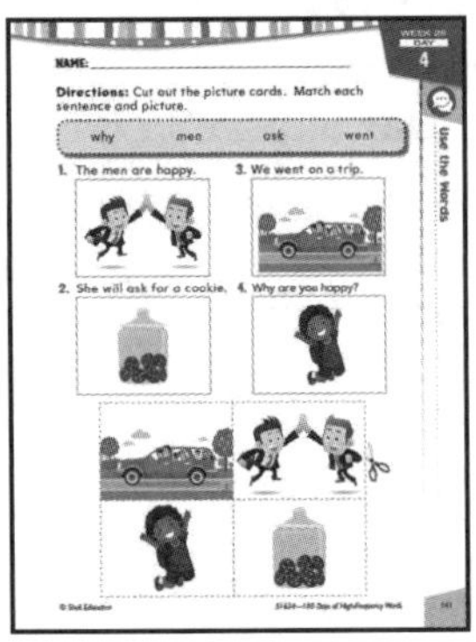

Week 26: Day 5 (page 142)

The men went to ask for food.

Week 27: Day 2 (page 144)

1. land
2. need
3. read
4. different

Week 28: Day 2 (page 149)

move	home	try	us
𝍷𝍷	𝍷𝍷𝍷	𝍸	𝍸𝍷

Week 28: Day 4 (page 151)

Week 28: Day 5 (page 152)

They will move us to a new home.

Week 29: Day 3 (page 155)

1. again
2. picture
3. hand
4. kind

Week 30: Day 2 (page 159)

1. play
2. off
3. spell
4. change

Week 30: Day 4 (page 161)

Week 30: Day 5 (page 162)

She went off to play.

Week 31: Day 2 (page 164)

away	house	animal	air
𝍸𝍷	𝍸	𝍷𝍷𝍷	𝍷𝍷

Week 32: Day 3 (page 170)

1. point
2. mother
3. letter
4. page

Week 33: Day 2 (page 174)

1. still
2. found
3. study
4. answer

Week 33: Day 4 (page 176)

Week 34: Day 2 (page 179)

every	learn	should	world
𝍷𝍷	𝍸	𝍸𝍷	𝍷𝍷𝍷

Week 35: Day 4 (page 186)

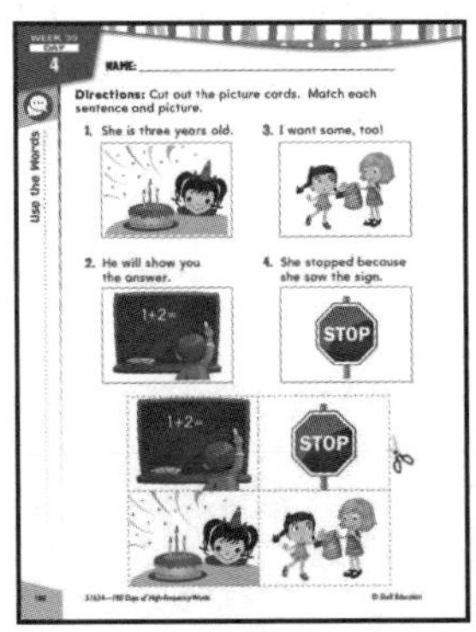

ANSWER KEY *(cont.)*

Week 36: Day 2 (page 189)

1. why
2. here
3. try
4. should

Week 36: Day 3 (page 190)

1. try
2. here
3. should
4. why

HOME/SCHOOL CONNECTIONS AND EXTENSION ACTIVITIES

Pages 198–205 can be used as home/school connection activities for additional practice or classroom extension activities. All game sheets have been left blank so the teacher can differentiate for each individual student and/or group in the class. The flash cards on pages 206–215 can be used as game cards, as well as student-facing assessment cards for quarterly assessments.

BINGO

Write the high-frequency words of the week (or ones that need to be practiced) on the BINGO board. Select a word from the deck of flash cards. Any player who has the word can place a chip on it. The first player to make a straight line calls out "Bingo!"

		FREE SPACE		

HOME/SCHOOL CONNECTIONS AND EXTENSION ACTIVITIES *(cont.)*

Race to 20! Race to 30!

Give each student a whiteboard or note pad to serve as a scoreboard. Use the flash cards from pages 206–215 to create a card pile for this game. Pick a card from the flash card pile, read the word, and count the letters in the word. Add a tally mark for each letter. Take turns picking cards, reading words, and adding up tally marks. The first player to reach 20 tally marks wins! As a challenge, Race to 30!

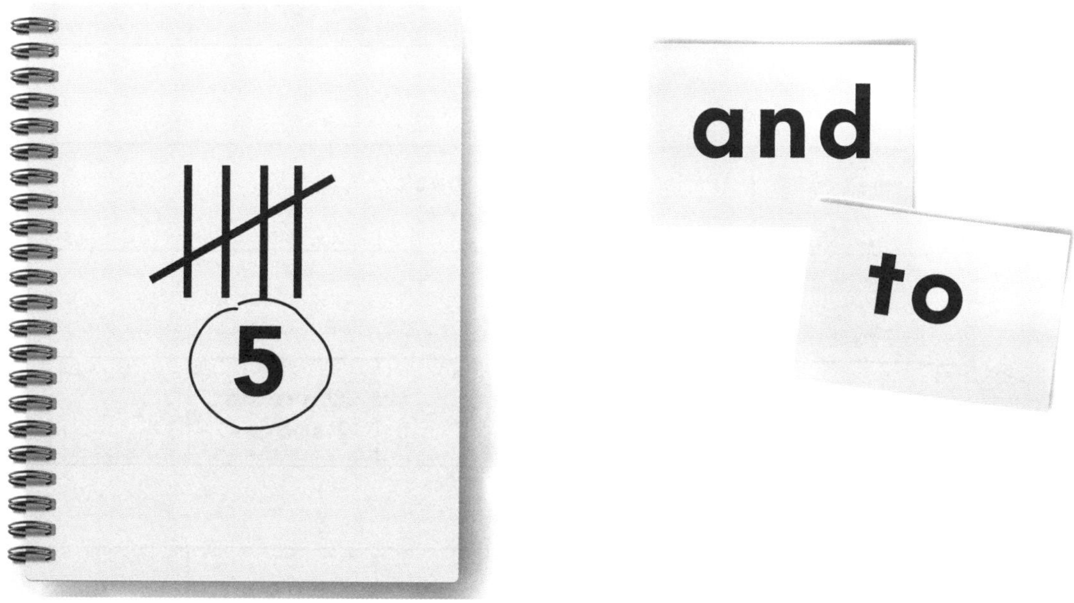

HOME/SCHOOL CONNECTIONS AND EXTENSION ACTIVITIES *(cont.)*

Word Board Game

Choose several words and place those flash cards in a pile. Write the words multiple times on the game board until all spaces are filled. Then, distribute a chip to each player. Have each player select a flash card, count the number of letters in the word, and then move his or her chip that number of spaces. Have students read every space they land on. The first player to reach the finish line wins!

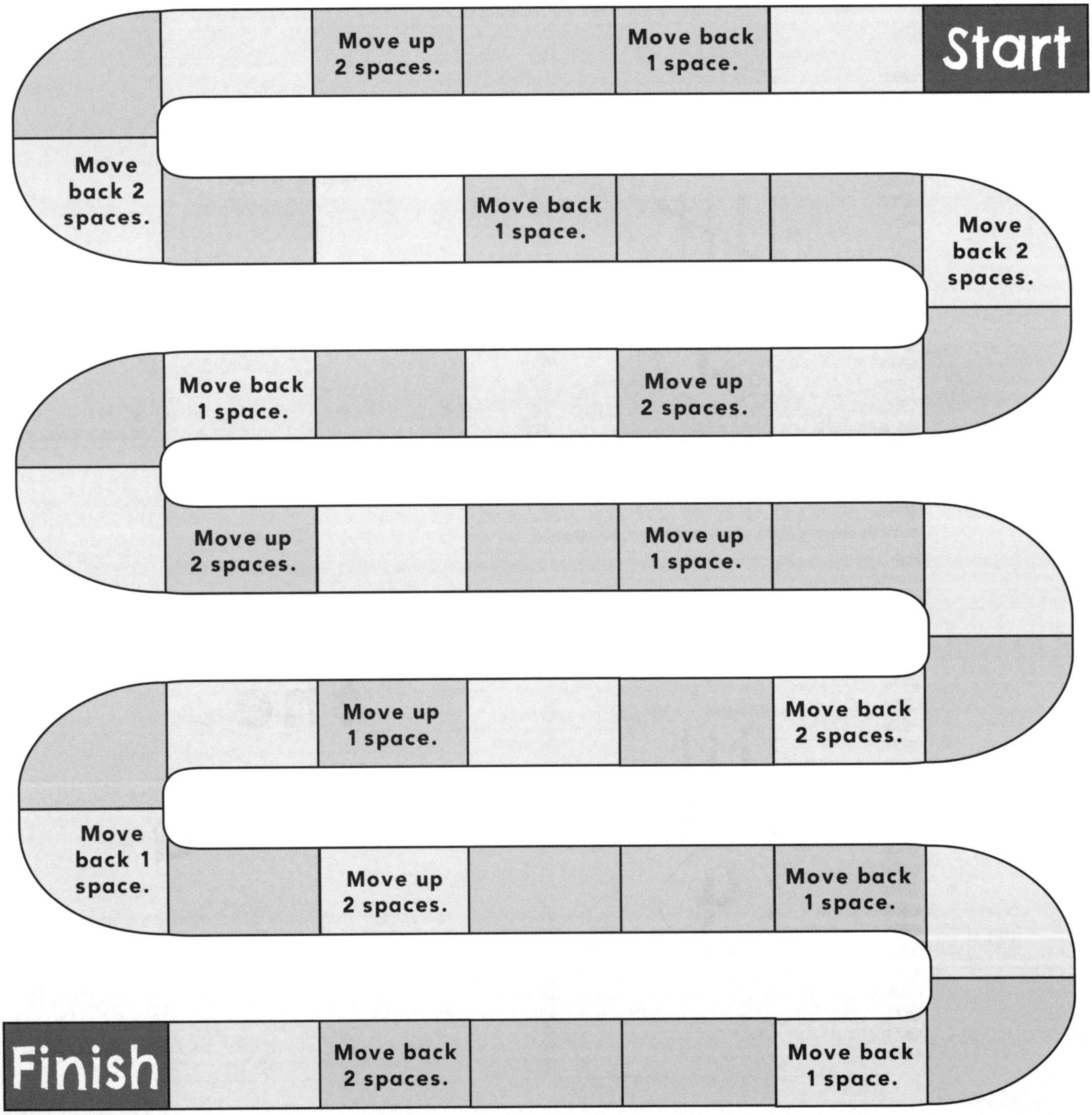

HOME/SCHOOL CONNECTIONS AND EXTENSION ACTIVITIES *(cont.)*

Word Bar Graph

Write the words of the week multiple times in the spinner. Write the words of the week on the lines at the bottom of the graph.

Use a paper clip and pencil to make a pointer. Place the paper clip in the middle of the spinner. Put the pencil inside of the paper clip so when it is spun, the paper clip circles around the pencil.

Have each student will spin the pointer and read the word that the paper clip lands on. Starting from the box above the word, fill in one box each time the pointer lands on that word. Play until one column reaches the top.

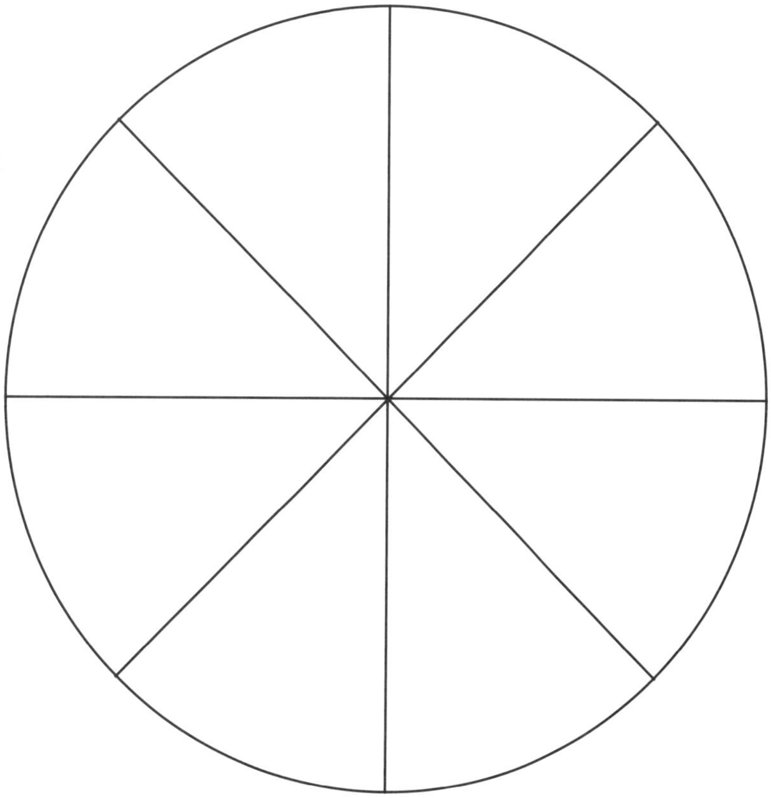

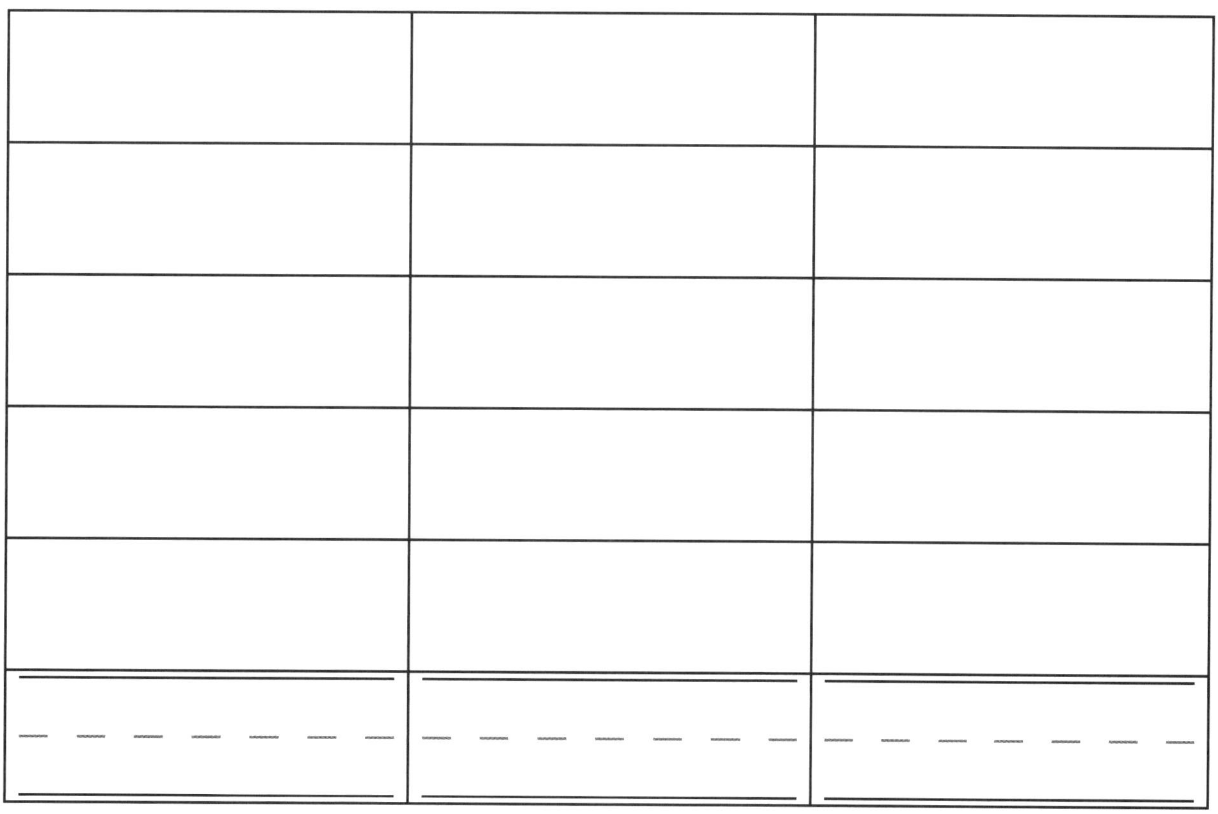

HOME/SCHOOL CONNECTIONS AND EXTENSION ACTIVITIES *(cont.)*

Tally It Up!

Select six words, and write them in the second column. Have each student roll a die 20 times. For each roll, students say the word associated with each number, then color one tally mark. For each roll have students color one box next to the word that matches the number rolled. To liven up the game, instruct students to say each word in a normal voice and a strange one.

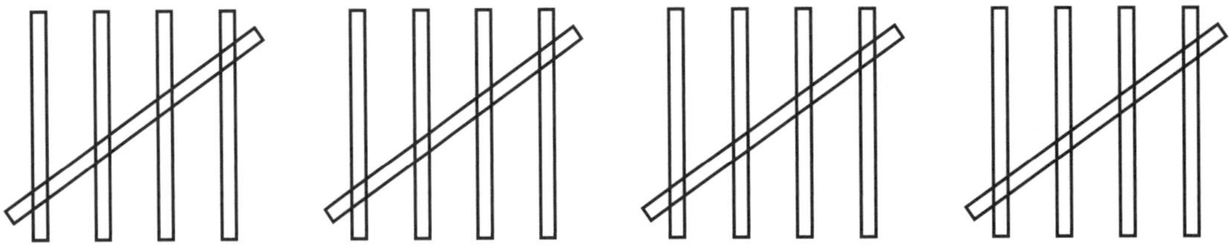

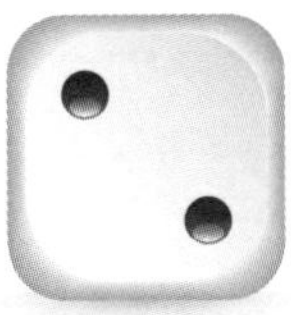									
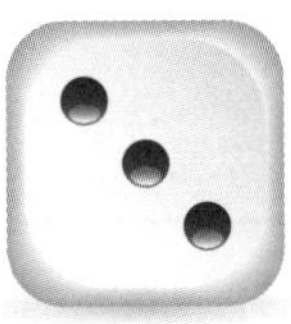									

HOME/SCHOOL CONNECTIONS AND EXTENSION ACTIVITIES *(cont.)*

Scavenger Hunt for the Print Rich Classroom

Have students take a classroom walk to find some of the words of the week. When students find a word, have them stand next to it. This game can be differentiated to include the following hunts:

- Find a word in the classroom that starts with the same sound as . . .
- Find a word in the classroom that ends with the same sound as . . .
- Find a word in the classroom that starts/ends with the same letter as . . .
- Find a word in the classroom that has the same syllable count as . . .
- Find a word in the classroom that has the same amount of letters as . . .
- Find a word in the classroom that has the same about of vowels/consonants as . . .

Tiny-Print Word Search

Use the chart below to find the high-frequency words of the week. Give each student a magnifying glass. Use the list on page 11 to call out each high-frequency word. **Note:** All of the words in this book are listed below multiple times!

that	may	from	could	are	there	want	name	year	they	was	very	for	try	spell	use
new	was	know	around	very	new	came	with	know	about	turn	boy	too	why	play	after
some	over	thing	over	went	such	little	much	big	again	think	first	put	move	three	men
where	use	small	their	place	some	picture	read	they	must	change	set	give	should	every	old
first	take	after	tell	for	us	were	may	same	could	every	mother	does	kind	air	off
home	kind	from	work	try	page	study	show	hand	follow	because	what	even	here	found	here
with	come	our	what	our	same	line	very	one	want	their	another	big	picture	away	write
say	back	try	ask	where	have	our	take	work	who	farm	learn	follow	because	letter	why
also	need	would	great	line	through	would	end	any	came	animal	right	such	again	house	point
most	little	even	been	move	know	should	why	great	land	are	does	spell	show	answer	ask
because	were	thing	good	another	much	why	been	sound	three	that	said	because	hand	animal	men
said	air	found	one	sentence	find	right	our	there	also	how	well	three	three	study	here
place	sound	who	world	well	help	just	me	any	letter	set	over	here	change	mother	went
have	give	live	about	sentence	before	come	right	play	around	through	large	home	want	still	read
away	how	just	man	want	mean	over	where	tell	back	small	only	new	off	page	need
year	live	only	good	say	too	man	where	want	two	put	find	turn	want	found	that
two	most	name	should	write	house	know	right	boy	different	still	before	us	learn	point	land
me	very	answer	think	help	farm	new	old	large	show	end	must	turn	world	every	different

HOME/SCHOOL CONNECTIONS AND EXTENSION ACTIVITIES *(cont.)*

Guess my Word

Print the flash cards on pages 206–215. Have students work in pairs. One partner should hold a flash card to his or her forehead while the other partner gives the clues. Once the partner guesses the word correctly, the other student takes a turn. Students can use any of the prompts below as clues:

- Use the word in a sentence, for example "I went to _______ party."
- "The word has _____ syllables."
- "The word rhymes with ______."
- "The word has _____ vowels."
- "The word has ____ consonants."

Dance and Write

Give every pair of students a dry-erase board and marker. Play some music. When the music stops, call out a word. The first team to write the word on their board and hold it up gets the point.

Dance, Tally, and Graph

As an alternative to Dance and Write, remove the competitive aspect. Give every student a clipboard and a sheet of paper. Have students write the words of the week on their paper. Play music, and when the music stops call out a word. Have students write a tally mark next to every word called. When students reach five tally marks for every word, repeat the game/song.

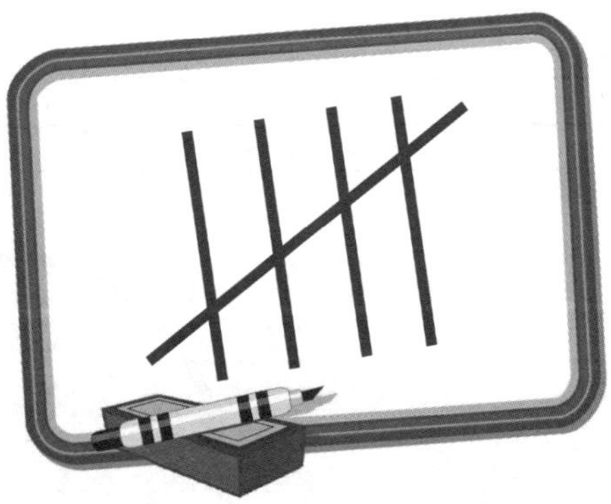

HOME/SCHOOL CONNECTIONS AND EXTENSION ACTIVITIES *(cont.)*

Ice Cream Word Sort

Choose a sorting category for students, and write it on the cone. Using the flash cards from pages 206–215, have students select and write words that fit the sort onto each scoop of ice cream. Have students color the ice cream once complete. Sorting categories can be found on pages 203–204.

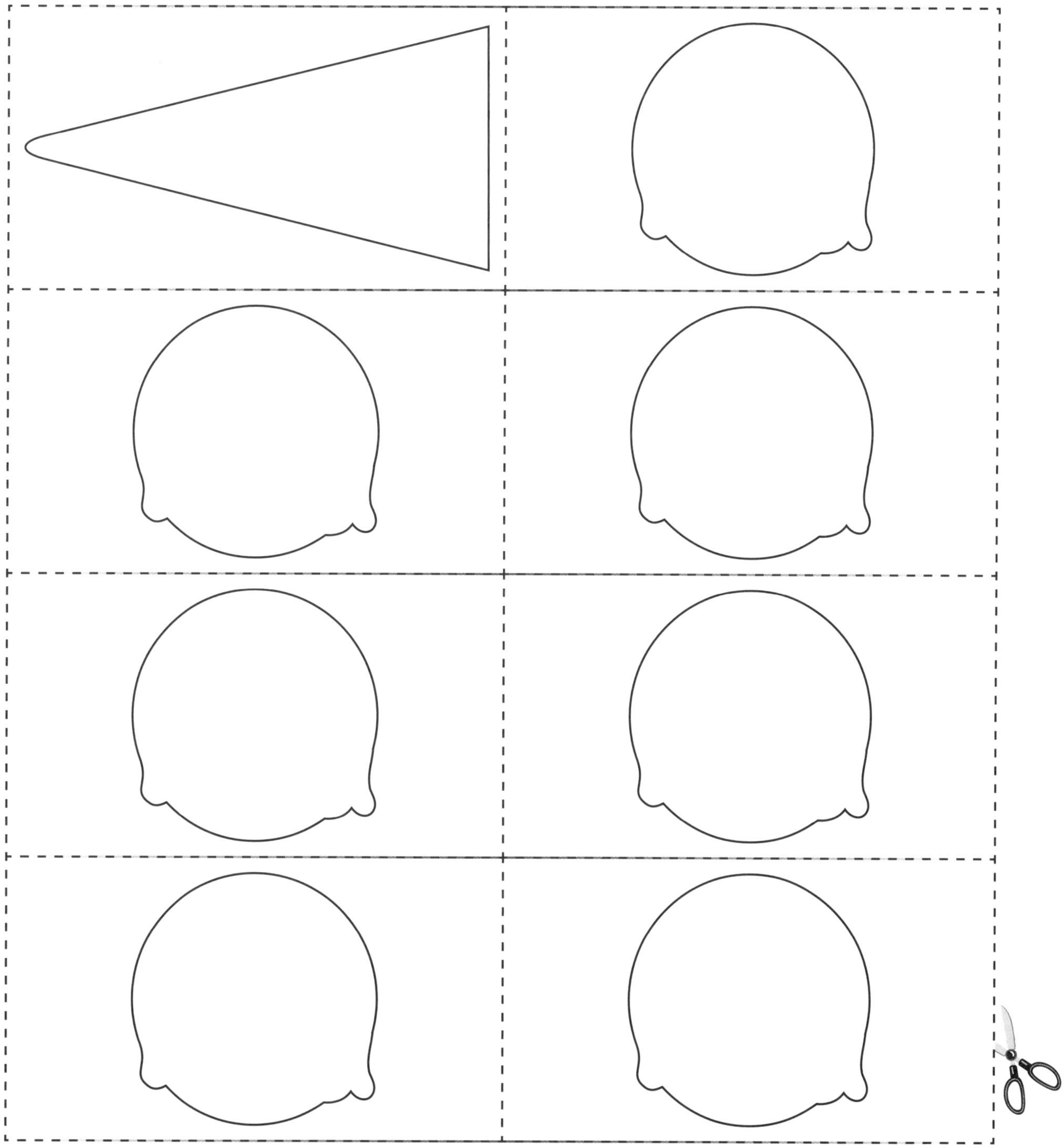

HIGH-FREQUENCY WORDS FLASH CARDS

The flash cards on pages 206–215 are organized by week. **Note:** If you are using the cards for the student diagnostic assessment, have students read the words left to right, as they would read text in a book. Below you will find weeks 1–3.

are	from	were
for	have	said
one	they	what
that	with	was

HIGH-FREQUENCY WORDS FLASH CARDS *(cont.)*

Below you will find weeks 4–7.

about	two	been	who
use	some	first	come
how	would	could	may
there	their	write	find

HIGH-FREQUENCY WORDS FLASH CARDS *(cont.)*

Below you will find weeks 8–10.

sound	work	me
take	little	year
new	know	place
over	only	most

HIGH-FREQUENCY WORDS FLASH CARDS *(cont.)*

Below you will find weeks 11–14.

very	just	man	say
give	thing	good	sentence
live	our	great	where
back	after	name	think

HIGH-FREQUENCY WORDS FLASH CARDS *(cont.)*

Below you will find weeks 15–17.

before	right	very
much	line	new
through	too	know
help	mean	over

HIGH-FREQUENCY WORDS FLASH CARDS *(cont.)*

Below you will find weeks 18–21.

through	tell	came	farm
where	any	want	show
right	same	follow	around
our	old	boy	also

HIGH-FREQUENCY WORDS FLASH CARDS *(cont.)*

Below you will find weeks 22–24.

small	well	big
put	does	even
set	another	must
three	end	large

HIGH-FREQUENCY WORDS FLASH CARDS *(cont.)*

Below you will find weeks 25–28.

turn	went	different	move
here	men	land	try
because	ask	need	us
such	why	read	home

HIGH-FREQUENCY WORDS FLASH CARDS *(cont.)*

Below you will find weeks 29–32.

hand	play	animal	letter
again	spell	house	point
picture	off	away	page
kind	change	air	mother

HIGH-FREQUENCY WORDS FLASH CARDS *(cont.)*

Below you will find weeks 33–36.

found	learn	because	why
still	world	show	should
study	should	three	try
answer	every	want	here

REFERENCES CITED

Fry, Edward. 2000. *1,000 Instant Words: The Most Common Words for Teaching Reading, Writing, and Spelling.* Huntington Beach, CA: Teacher Created Materials.

Marzano, Robert. 2010. "When Practice Makes Perfect…Sense." *Educational Leadership* 68 (3): 81–83.

McIntosh, Margaret E. 1997. "Formative Assessment in Mathematics." *The Clearing House: A Journal of Educational Strategies* 71 (2): 92–96.

US Department of Health and Human Services. 2000. *Report of the National Reading Panel: Teaching Children to Read: An Evidence-Based Assessment of the Scientific Research Literature on Reading and its Implications for Reading Instruction.* Washington, DC: US Government Printing Office.

CONTENTS OF THE DIGITAL RESOURCES

Teacher Resources

Resource	PDF Filename	Microsoft Word® Filename
Daily Descriptions	daily.pdf	daily.docx
Activity Descriptions	activity.pdf	activity.docx
Student Item Analysis Checklist	studentlog.pdf	studentlog.docx
Class Item Analysis	classlog.pdf	classlog.docx
Standards Chart	standards.pdf	

Student Resources

Resource	PDF Filename
BINGO Board	bingo.pdf
Word Board Game	boardgame.pdf
Word Bar Graph	wordgraph.pdf
Spinner	spinner.pdf
Tally It Up!	tally.pdf
Tiny Word Search	tinysearch.pdf
Ice Cream Sort	icecream.pdf
High-Frequency Words Flash Cards	flashcards.pdf